Maher Asaad Baker

Colors of the Kingdom

Contents

Introduction

Thailand is a nation with a rich and diverse cultural and artistic heritage. Situated in Southeast Asia, between influential neighbors, it has embraced a variety of creative expressions that meld indigenous traditions with external influences, resulting in a captivating and unique identity.

In exploring Thailand's artistic heritage, we will journey through time, examining the diverse art forms that have flourished in this fascinating country. From the ancient temples steeped in history to the modern galleries brimming with creativity, we will witness the evolution of Thai art while still honoring its deep-rooted connections.

Through this expedition, we seek to offer insight into Thailand's vibrant culture and rich history, providing opportunities for appreciation and learning. By delving into the world of Thai art, we can gain an understanding of the country's aesthetic achievements and a profound appreciation for its distinct identity.

Thailand has a rich artistic heritage encompasses a wide range of disciplines and mediums, from traditional painting, sculpture, and architecture to textiles, pottery, and performing arts. This diversity results from the nation's unique geographical and historical position, allowing it to absorb influences from its neighbors and beyond.

The history of Thailand's artistic heritage dates back thousands of years, to the early days of human civilization in Southeast Asia. The region's first inhabitants left behind a rich archaeological record that demonstrates their artistic abilities. Excavations at sites such as Ban Chiang and Ban Non-Wat have revealed a variety of artifacts, including pottery, jewelry, and metalwork, showcasing the creativity and sophistication of these early societies. These ancient artisans laid the foundations for the artistic traditions that would thrive in the centuries to come.

As Thailand's artistic evolution progressed, the influences of Indian, Khmer, and Chinese cultures played a significant role. In the first millennium CE, the arrival of Indian traders and missionaries led to a cultural exchange, introducing Southeast Asia to the religious, philosophical, and artistic traditions of the Indian subcontinent. This exchange had a lasting impact on Thailand's artistic landscape as local artisans started integrating Indian motifs, techniques, and iconography into their work, resulting in a unique fusion of indigenous and foreign elements that came to define Thailand's cultural identity.

One notable result of this synthesis can be seen in Thai architecture, where the influence of Indian and Khmer styles is evident in the design and ornamentation of both religious and secular structures. The towering spires of Thai temples, or wats, reflect the enduring legacy of Indian architectural principles, emphasizing the vertical axis as a symbolic link between the earthly and divine realms. Additionally, the intricate bas-reliefs and sculptures adorning these sacred structures demonstrate the assimilation of Indian and Khmer artistic traditions, featuring depictions of Hindu and Buddhist deities, mythical creatures, and epic narratives.

The Khmer Empire, which ruled over much of mainland Southeast Asia from the 9th to the 13th centuries, deeply influenced the artistic development of Thailand. The architectural and sculptural legacy of the Khmer can be observed in the impressive ruins of ancient cities such as Phimai and Phanom Rung, showcasing the grandeur and sophistication of Khmer art and architecture. The Khmer influence is particularly noticeable in the design of Thai temples and palaces, which often feature a cruciform plan with a central tower or prang surrounded by subsidiary structures. The intricate decorations of these buildings, including elaborate carvings and friezes, further reflect the Khmer's impact on Thai artistic expression.

The influence of China on Thai art, although not as strong as that of India and Khmer, is still significant, especially in ceramics and textiles. The long history of trade and cultural exchange between China and Southeast Asia allowed the transfer of Chinese artistic techniques and motifs, which were eagerly adopted and adjusted by Thai artists. The result was a vibrant mix of Chinese and local elements, visible in the beautiful porcelain produced at kiln sites like Sisatchanalai and Sukhothai, and in the luxurious silk textiles woven in the royal workshops of Ayutthaya and Bangkok.

The Sukhothai and Ayutthaya kingdoms, which prospered from the 13th to the 18th centuries, represent crucial periods in Thailand's artistic history. The Sukhothai Kingdom, often called the "dawn of Thai civilization," was marked by significant cultural and artistic growth as the emerging Thai nation aimed to establish a distinct identity amid external influences. The art of this era is characterized by an elegant and refined aesthetic, with a particular focus on the human form. The sculptures of the Sukhothai period, featuring graceful lines, delicate features, and serene expressions, are considered some of the finest examples of Thai artistic achievement.

The Ayutthaya Kingdom, which followed Sukhothai as the leading power in the region, continued and expanded the artistic traditions established by its predecessor. The Ayutthaya period is characterized by a greater emphasis on grandeur and opulence, as the kingdom aimed to demonstrate its power and prestige through its artistic and architectural endeavors. The temples and palaces of Ayutthaya, known for their impressive scale and lavish decoration, stand as a testament to the artistic ambitions of the era. The art of this period also exhibits a greater degree of realism and naturalism, as evidenced in the detailed and lifelike depictions of animals, plants, and human figures in painting and sculpture.

The significance of art in Thai society cannot be overstated, as it permeates every aspect of the nation's cultural and spiritual life. Art is not just a form of aesthetic expression or a means of adornment, but rather a deeply ingrained and integral component of Thai identity. From the elaborate rituals and ceremonies that punctuate the religious calendar to the intricate craftsmanship of everyday objects, art is woven into the very fabric of Thai society.

In the realm of religion, art acts as a powerful medium for conveying spiritual principles and beliefs, and as a way to enable connection with the divine. The intricate embellishment of temples and religious objects, with their rich symbolism and imagery, creates a sacred environment for worshippers to participate in acts of reverence and introspection. The creation of religious art is also viewed as a way to accumulate spiritual merit and karmic benefits through artistic expression.

Preserving traditional artistic techniques and knowledge is highly valued in Thai society as it ensures the continuation and vitality of the nation's cultural legacy. The passing down of artistic skills and knowledge often occurs within families, ensuring the survival of age-old techniques and customs through generations. Additionally, the Thai government has made efforts to protect the nation's artistic heritage by establishing institutions such as the National Museum and the Fine Arts Department, dedicated to conserving, promoting, and studying Thai art.

In today's world, Thai artists are facing the challenges and opportunities brought by globalization and modernity as they strive to reinterpret and reinvent traditional art forms in a rapidly changing global landscape. This process of artistic reinvention is not new but continues the long-standing tradition of cultural synthesis and adaptation that has shaped Thailand's artistic development.

Contemporary Thai artists are exploring a wide range of themes and issues, including social and political upheavals, environmental concerns, and technological advancements. They are experimenting with new mediums and techniques, incorporating elements of popular culture and global art movements, and pushing the boundaries of traditional artistic norms. In doing so, they are creating a new artistic style rooted in Thailand's cultural heritage while embracing global artistic influences.

Thailand's art heritage is a valuable cultural asset that deserves to be preserved and promoted. It is a testament to the country's rich cultural history and an essential part of its national identity. As we navigate the complexities of the modern world, we must protect this heritage while also encouraging its development and adaptation. By combining preservation efforts, educational initiatives, and cultural exchange, we can ensure that Thailand's art heritage continues to thrive and inspire future generations.

The path ahead may have challenges, but with a dedicated commitment to cultural preservation and a willingness to embrace innovation, the future of Thailand's art heritage is set to be as vibrant and captivating as its glorious past. This is a journey that requires our collective effort and engagement, as the preservation of art heritage is not just a cultural duty; it is an investment in our shared human legacy.

Historical Foundations

The origins of Thai art can be traced back to prehistoric times, as archaeological findings offer valuable insights into the artistic expressions of ancient Thai civilizations. The earliest forms of art in Thailand included cave paintings, pottery, and sculptures, which were used by people to convey their beliefs, experiences, and cultural identities.

Cave paintings found in different parts of Thailand, like Pha Taem National Park and Tham Pha Nang Khoi, demonstrate the artistic skills of prehistoric inhabitants. These paintings, mostly made using red and white pigments, depict a variety of themes, including human figures, animals, and geometric patterns. The human figures are often shown in different activities such as dancing, hunting, and fishing, reflecting the daily lives of ancient Thai people. The animal motifs mostly feature wild animals like elephants, deer, and tigers, which may have held symbolic significance in the cultural and religious practices of prehistoric Thai societies.

Pottery also played a significant role as an artistic expression during this time. The earliest pottery found in Thailand dates back to the Neolithic era and is characterized by simple forms and rough textures. However, as pottery-making techniques evolved, the pottery became more sophisticated, featuring intricate designs and motifs. The pottery discovered in Ban Chiang recognized as a UNESCO World Heritage site, is a prime example of the advanced pottery-making techniques of prehistoric Thai people. It is characterized by its distinctive red-on-buff ware, adorned with elaborate geometric patterns and human and animal motifs.

During the prehistoric period in Thailand, sculptures became a prominent form of artistic expression. The earliest sculptures found in Thailand are mainly made of stone and depict human figures and animals. The sculptures of human figures are characterized by stylized forms and exaggerated features, possibly serving a symbolic or ritualistic purpose. On the other hand, animal sculptures are often depicted in a more naturalistic manner, likely influenced by the surrounding environment and the fauna of that time.

The neighboring civilizations, such as Dvaravati, Srivijaya, and Khmer, had a significant impact on the development of Thai art, influencing artistic techniques, styles, and iconography.

The Dvaravati civilization, which thrived in central Thailand from the 6th to the 11th century, played a crucial role in shaping Thai art. As a predominantly Buddhist civilization, the religious beliefs and practices of the people heavily influenced the art forms of that era. Dvaravati art is characterized by a distinctive style, combining Indian and local artistic traditions. Examples of Dvaravati art include Buddha images, known for their serene expressions, elongated earlobes, and stylized drapery. Additionally, Dvaravati art features various motifs, such as mythical creatures, floral patterns, and geometric designs, often integrated into the architectural elements of Buddhist temples and shrines.

The Srivijaya civilization, which thrived in present-day southern Thailand and Sumatra from the 7th to the 13th century, was a maritime trading power that had extensive contacts with India, China, and other Southeast Asian civilizations. The Srivijaya civilization played a significant role in spreading Buddhism in Southeast Asia, and the religious beliefs and practices of the people had a profound impact on the art forms of that era. Srivijaya art is characterized by a unique style that fuses Indian, Chinese, and local artistic traditions. The most notable examples of Srivijaya art are the Buddha images, known for their serene expressions, elongated earlobes, and stylized drapery. Srivijaya art also includes various motifs such as mythical creatures, floral patterns, and geometric designs, which were often integrated into the architectural elements of Buddhist temples and shrines.

The Khmer civilization, which thrived in present-day Cambodia from the 9th to the 15th century, had a substantial influence on

Thai art development. The Khmer civilization was predominantly Hindu, but Buddhism also played a significant role in the religious beliefs and practices of the people. Khmer art is known for its unique style, combining Indian and local artistic traditions. The most notable examples of Khmer art are the grand architectural structures, such as temples and palaces, distinguished by their massive scale, detailed carvings, and intricate ornamentation. Khmer art also includes various motifs like mythical creatures, floral patterns, and geometric designs, often integrated into the architectural elements of temples and palaces.

Religion, particularly Buddhism and Hinduism, had a profound impact on the early forms, symbols, and rituals of Thai art. The religious beliefs and practices significantly influenced the iconography and aesthetics of Thai art, as well as the function and purpose of artistic expressions.

Buddhism, which originated in India in the 6th century BCE, had a profound impact on the development of Thai art. The religious beliefs and practices of Buddhism, such as the Four Noble Truths and the Eightfold Path, provided a framework for the artistic expressions of the Thai people. The Buddha images are the most prominent examples of Thai art and serve as a visual representation of the Buddha's teachings and the path to enlightenment. These images are characterized by their serene expressions, elongated earlobes, and stylized drapery, which allude to the Buddha's renunciation of worldly pleasures and his attainment of enlightenment. The Buddhist temples and shrines were adorned with intricate carvings and elaborate ornamentation to enhance the spiritual experience of the worshippers.

Hinduism, which originated in India in the 2nd millennium BCE, also had a significant impact on the development of Thai art. The religious beliefs and practices of Hinduism, such as the concept of dharma and the worship of deities, provided a framework for the artistic expressions of the Thai people. The Hindu deities, such as Vishnu, Shiva, and Brahma, were often depicted in Thai art, either as individual figures or as part of a larger narrative scene. The Hindu temples and shrines, which were centers of religious worship and artistic expression, were adorned with intricate carvings and elaborate ornamentation to enhance the spiritual experience of the worshippers.

Temples, shrines, and religious structures played a significant role in the development of Thai art. These structures served as the centers of religious worship and artistic expression. They provided a platform for the artistic expression of the Thai people, such as the creation of Buddha images, murals, and sculptures. The temples and shrines were adorned with intricate carvings and elaborate ornamentation, which enhanced the spiritual experience of the worshippers. These artistic expressions also served to reinforce the religious beliefs and practices of the people, as well as the cultural and social dynamics of the ancient Thai civilizations.

The origins of Thai art can be traced back to the prehistoric epoch, where archaeological remnants provide insight into the artistic expressions of the ancient Thai civilizations. The development of Thai art was significantly influenced by neighboring civilizations, such as Dvaravati, Srivijaya, and Khmer, shaping the early Thai art forms, symbols, and rituals. Religion, particularly Buddhism and Hinduism, played a significant role in shaping the iconography and aesthetics of Thai art, as well as the function and purpose of the artistic expressions. These beliefs and practices had a profound impact on the development of Thai art.

Traditional Music

The melodious sounds of Thailand's traditional music have been captivating listeners for centuries. This rich musical heritage has evolved, influenced by various cultural and historical factors. To truly appreciate the beauty and complexity of traditional Thai music, it is essential to understand its origins and development.

The history of Thai music can be traced back to ancient times, with evidence of musical instruments and performances found in archaeological sites dating back to the Bronze

Age. The earliest forms of Thai music were likely used for religious ceremonies and rituals, as well as for entertainment during communal gatherings.

As Thailand's cultural and political landscape evolved, so too did its music. The Mon and Khmer civilizations, which flourished in present-day Thailand before the arrival of the Thai people, had a significant impact on the development of Thai music. The Mon, in particular, is credited with introducing Buddhism to Thailand, which brought with it new forms of religious music.

The establishment of the Sukhothai Kingdom in the 13th century marked the beginning of the Thai cultural identity, and with it, the development of a distinctly Thai musical tradition. During this period, the royal court played a crucial role in the patronage and development of music. Court musicians were highly respected and skilled in performing a variety of musical genres, from classical court music to folk music.

The Ayutthaya Kingdom, which succeeded the Sukhothai Kingdom in the 14th century, saw the continued development of Thai music. The Ayutthaya period was marked by increased contact with foreign cultures, including those of India, China, and Persia. These cultural exchanges had a profound impact on Thai music, with new instruments, techniques, and styles being introduced and incorporated into the existing musical tradition.

The modern era of Thai music began in the late 19th century, with the establishment of the Chakri Dynasty and the modernization of Thailand. During this period, Western musical influences began to make their way into Thailand, with the introduction of new instruments such as the piano and violin. Western musical notation was also adopted, which facilitated the transcription and preservation of traditional Thai music.

Despite these Western influences, traditional Thai music continued to thrive and evolve. In the 20th century, Thai musicians began to experiment with new forms and styles, incorporating elements of jazz, pop, and rock into their music. This fusion of traditional and contemporary styles has resulted in a vibrant and diverse musical landscape that continues to captivate audiences today.

Traditional Thai music is characterized by its use of a wide range of musical instruments, each with its own unique sound and cultural significance. Some of the most important instruments in Thai music include:

Khim: The khim is a type of dulcimer, consisting of a trapezoidal soundboard with metal strings stretched across it. The khim is played by striking the strings with two light bamboo hammers, producing a bright, resonant sound. The khim is often used in classical Thai music, as well as in folk music and religious ceremonies.

Ranad: The ranad is a type of xylophone, consisting of a series of wooden bars of varying lengths suspended over a resonator. The ranad is played by striking the bars with two mallets, producing a clear, melodic sound. The ranad is a key instrument in classical Thai music, as well as in folk music and religious ceremonies.

Sueng: The sueng is a type of plucked lute, consisting of a long, narrow neck and a round, hollow body. The sueng has four strings, which are plucked with a plectrum made of horn or plastic. The sueng is used in both classical and folk music and is particularly associated with the music of the Isan region in northeastern Thailand.

Traditional Thai music encompasses a wide range of forms and styles, each with its own unique characteristics and cultural significance. Some of the most important forms and styles of Thai music include:

Classical Court Music: Classical court music is a highly structured and formalized genre of Thai music, performed by ensembles of musicians in the royal court. This music is characterized by its complex melodies and rhythms, as well as its use of traditional Thai instruments such as the khim, ranad, and sueng.

Folk Music: Folk music is a diverse and vibrant genre of Thai music, performed by rural communities throughout Thailand. This music is characterized by its use of traditional instruments and its focus on local themes and stories. Folk music is often performed during festivals and other communal gatherings and serves as a means of preserving and celebrating local cultural traditions.

Religious Music: Religious music plays an important role in Thai culture, particularly within the context of Buddhism. This music is used in various religious ceremonies and rituals, such as alms-giving ceremonies and temple festivals. Religious music often features the use of traditional instruments and chants and serves to create a sense of sacredness and reverence.

The Melodic Sounds of Classical Thai Music

Classical Thai music is a highly structured and formalized genre of music, characterized by its complex melodies and rhythms. This music is often performed by ensembles of musicians, using a variety of traditional Thai instruments such as the khim, ranad, and sueng.

Piphat is a type of classical Thai music performed by an ensemble of musicians. This music is characterized by its complex melodies and rhythms, as well as its use of traditional Thai instruments. The piphat ensemble typically consists of a khim, ranad, sueng, and other instruments such as the pi (a type of oboe) and the klong (a set of tuned drums).

There are several different types of piphat, each with its unique characteristics. For example, piphat mai nuam is a slow and stately form of piphat, often performed during royal ceremonies and processions. Piphat mai khaek, on the other hand, is a faster and more lively form of piphat, influenced by Persian and Indian musical traditions.

Khruang sai is a type of classical Thai music that features vocal performances accompanied by an ensemble of musicians. This music is characterized by its complex melodies and rhythms, as well as its use of traditional Thai instruments.

There are several different types of khruang sai, each with its unique characteristics. For example, khruang sai luk thung is a form of khruang sai that features singing in the luk thung style, a popular genre of Thai music characterized by its use of traditional Thai instruments and its focus on rural themes and stories. Khruang sai mor lam, on the other hand, is a form of khruang sai that features singing in the mor lam style, a traditional genre of music from the Isan region in northeastern Thailand.

Throughout its history, classical Thai music has been shaped and enriched by the contributions of numerous talented musicians and composers. Some of the most renowned figures in the world of classical Thai music include:

Luang Pradit Phairoh (1905-1993): Luang Pradit Phairoh was a renowned Thai musician and composer, known for his contributions to the development of classical Thai music in the 20th century. He was a master of the khim and the ranad and composed numerous works for these instruments.

Somtow Sucharitkul (born 1952): Somtow Sucharitkul is a Thai-American composer and conductor, known for his contributions to the world of classical music. He has composed numerous works for orchestra, as well as operas and ballets. His music often incorporates elements of traditional Thai music, as well as other Asian musical traditions.

Payap Pongpat (born 1953): Payap Pongpat is a Thai musician and composer, known for his contributions to the world of classical Thai music. He is a master of the sueng and has composed numerous works for this instrument. He has also conducted extensive research into the history and theory of traditional Thai music.

Preserving the Traditions of Thai Folk Music

Thailand's rich musical heritage is not limited to its classical music tradition. The country is also home to a vibrant and diverse folk music scene, with each region boasting its unique sounds and styles.

Thai folk music is characterized by its use of traditional instruments and its focus on local themes and stories. Some of the most important regional folk music traditions in Thailand include:

Luk Thung: Luk thung is a popular genre of Thai music that originated in the central plains region of Thailand. This music is characterized by its use of traditional Thai instruments, such as the khim and the sueng, and its focus on rural themes and stories.

Mor Lam: Mor lam is a traditional genre of music from the Isan region in northeastern

Thailand. This music is characterized by its use of traditional Isan instruments, such as the khaen (a type of mouth organ) and the phin (a type of plucked lute), and its focus on local themes and stories.

Manora: Manora is a traditional genre of music and dance from southern Thailand. This music is characterized by its use of traditional southern Thai instruments, such as the ranad and the pi, and its focus on local myths and legends.

One of the key features of Thai folk music is its reliance on oral transmission. Many folk songs and melodies have been passed down through generations, with musicians learning their craft through observation and imitation rather than formal instruction.

This reliance on oral transmission has helped to preserve the rich musical heritage of Thailand's rural communities. However, it also poses challenges in terms of documenting and preserving this music for future generations. In recent years, efforts have been made to record and transcribe traditional Thai folk music, to ensure its continued survival.

Thai folk music continues to thrive and evolve in the modern era, with contemporary musicians and ensembles keeping these traditions alive through performances and recordings. Some notable contemporary folk musicians and ensembles include:

Carabao: Carabao is a popular Thai rock band that incorporates elements of traditional Thai music into their sound. The band's music often deals with social and political issues and has been influential in raising awareness of these issues in Thailand.

The Paradise Bangkok Molam International Band: The Paradise Bangkok Molam International Band is a Thai-American ensemble that specializes in the performance of mor lam music. The band's music combines traditional Isan instruments and melodies with contemporary musical styles, creating a unique and innovative sound.

Dao Bandon: Dao Bandon is a Thai folk singer and musician, known for her performances of traditional Thai folk songs. She has been instrumental in preserving and promoting Thai folk music and has performed at numerous festivals and events throughout Thailand.

Music plays an important role in Thai religious practices, particularly within the context of Buddhism. In Thai Buddhist ceremonies and rituals, music is used to create a sense of sacredness and reverence and to facilitate spiritual connection and contemplation.

Traditional Instruments and Chants in Buddhist Ceremonies

Traditional Thai musical instruments, such as the khim, ranad, and sueng, are often used in Buddhist ceremonies and rituals. These instruments are used to accompany chants and hymns, as well as to provide musical interludes during ceremonies.

Chanting is an important aspect of Thai Buddhist practice, and is used to recite sacred texts and to express devotion and reverence. Chants are often performed in a call-and-response format, with a lead chanter being joined by a chorus of other chanting monks or laypeople.

Music is used in Thai religious contexts to create a sense of sacredness and reverence.

This is achieved through the use of specific melodies, rhythms, and instruments, as well as through the performance of chants and hymns.

In Thai Buddhist temples, music is often used to create a peaceful and contemplative atmosphere, conducive to meditation and spiritual reflection. During alms-giving ceremonies, music is used to express gratitude and devotion and to create a sense of connection between the givers and receivers of alms.

There are numerous examples of music being used in Thai religious contexts. Some notable examples include:

The Royal Barge Procession: The Royal Barge Procession is an annual ceremony held in Bangkok, in which the king and other members of the royal family are transported along the Chao Phraya River in a procession of elaborately decorated barges. The procession is accompanied by traditional Thai music, performed by ensembles of musicians on board the barges.

The Kathin Ceremony: The Kathin Ceremony is an annual Buddhist ceremony held in Thailand, in which new robes and other necessities are donated to monks. During the ceremony, traditional Thai music is performed, and chants and hymns are recited.

The Songkran Festival: The Songkran Festival is a traditional Thai New Year celebration, held annually in April. During the festival, traditional Thai music is performed, and water is poured over Buddha images and the hands of elders as a sign of respect and blessing.

Calligraphy

Thai calligraphy has evolved over the centuries, drawing inspiration from various ancient scripts and cultural influences. This intricate form of artistic expression has played a significant role in shaping Thailand's cultural identity, leaving an indelible mark on both religious and secular contexts. To truly appreciate the beauty and complexity of Thai calligraphy, it is essential to understand its origins, historical context, and the techniques and styles that have developed over time.

The origins of Thai calligraphy can be traced back to ancient scripts such as Khmer and Indian influences, which laid the foundation for the development of this unique art form. The Khmer script, which was used in the Angkor period, had a significant impact on the early development of Thai calligraphy. As the Thai cultural identity began to take shape, the script evolved to reflect the distinct linguistic and aesthetic sensibilities of the Thai people.

Indian influences, particularly the Brahmi and Pallava scripts, also played a crucial role in shaping the early development of Thai calligraphy. These scripts, which were introduced to the region through trade and cultural exchange, provided a rich source of inspiration for Thai calligraphers. Over time, Thai calligraphy developed its distinctive style, characterized by its fluid lines, delicate curves, and intricate details.

Thai calligraphy has a rich and varied history, with its use spanning a wide range of contexts and purposes. In royal circles, calligraphy was used to create ornate and elaborate royal decrees, reflecting the power and prestige of the Thai monarchy. These decrees, which were often adorned with gold leaf and other decorative elements, served as a testament to the skill and artistry of Thai calligraphers.

In religious contexts, Thai calligraphy played an essential role in the transcription of sacred Buddhist texts. Monks and scholars, who were often skilled calligraphers, painstakingly copied these texts onto palm leaves or handmade paper, preserving the teachings of the Buddha for future generations. The act of writing these texts was considered a form of spiritual practice, with calligraphers imbuing each stroke with mindfulness and devotion.

Thai calligraphy is characterized by its delicate and intricate style, which requires a high level of skill and precision. One of the most celebrated styles of Thai calligraphy is the "Lai Thai" style, which is known for its elegant and refined aesthetic. This style, which is often used for religious texts and royal decrees, features elongated and sinuous lines, creating a sense of fluidity and grace.

Another important style of Thai calligraphy is the "Khom" style, which is influenced by the Khmer script. This style, which is characterized by its angular and geometric forms, is often used for inscriptions on stone and metal, as well as for decorative purposes.

Thai calligraphy has played a significant role in both religious and secular contexts, reflecting the diverse and multifaceted nature of Thai culture. In religious ceremonies, calligraphy is used to create sacred texts and scriptures, as well as to adorn temples and other religious spaces. The act of writing these texts is considered a form of spiritual practice, with calligraphers imbuing each stroke with mindfulness and devotion.

In secular contexts, Thai calligraphy has been used for a wide range of purposes, from decorative arts and signage to official documents and correspondence. The art form has also been adapted to suit modern contexts, with calligraphers incorporating digital tools and techniques to create innovative and contemporary designs.

The rich artistic heritage of Thai calligraphy has had a profound impact on contemporary art practices in Thailand. Many modern artists have drawn inspiration from traditional calligraphic techniques and styles, incorporating these elements into their work in innovative and imaginative ways.

One notable example of this fusion of traditional and contemporary styles can be seen in the work of Thai artist, Chumpol Taksapornchai. Taksapornchai, who is known for his intricate and detailed designs, combines traditional Thai calligraphy with modern graphic design elements, creating a unique and captivating visual language.

Other contemporary artists, such as Ajarn Saneh Sangsuk and Sompop Budtarad, have also explored the boundaries of Thai calligraphy, using the art form to delve into themes of identity, spirituality, and cultural heritage. These artists, who are part of a growing movement to preserve and promote Thai calligraphy, are helping to ensure that this vital aspect of Thailand's artistic heritage continues to thrive and evolve in the modern age.

As a vital part of Thailand's artistic heritage, Thai calligraphy must be preserved and promoted for future generations. Efforts to teach and promote Thai calligraphy in schools and universities, as well as in public spaces, are helping to foster greater appreciation for the art form among the general public.

Government initiatives and cultural organizations, such as the Thai Calligraphy Conservation Association and the National Library of Thailand, have played a crucial role in promoting Thai calligraphy as a national treasure. These organizations, which are dedicated to preserving and promoting Thailand's rich cultural heritage, have helped to raise awareness of the importance of Thai calligraphy and its role in shaping Thailand's artistic identity.

In recent years, there has been a resurgence of interest in Thai calligraphy, with schools and universities offering courses and workshops to teach the art form to a new generation of students. These educational initiatives, which are often led by master calligraphers and experienced teachers, provide students with the opportunity to learn the techniques and styles of Thai calligraphy, as well as to gain a deeper understanding of its historical and cultural significance.

The use of calligraphy in public spaces, such as murals, street art, and architectural design, has also helped to celebrate Thailand's cultural heritage and promote greater appreciation for the art form. In cities like Bangkok and Chiang Mai, calligraphic elements can be seen adorning the walls of temples, museums, and other public spaces, serving as a testament to the enduring beauty and relevance of Thai calligraphy.

Government initiatives and cultural organizations have played a vital role in promoting Thai calligraphy as a national treasure and fostering greater appreciation for the art form among the general public. Through exhibitions, workshops, and other educational events, these organizations have helped to raise awareness of the importance of Thai calligraphy and its role in shaping Thailand's artistic identity.

One notable example of this is the annual Thai Calligraphy Festival, which is organized by the Thai Calligraphy Conservation Association. This event, which brings together master calligraphers, artists, and enthusiasts from across the country, provides a platform for the exchange of ideas and techniques, as well as an opportunity to showcase the beauty and diversity of Thai calligraphy.

Calligraphy masters and cultural institutions in Thailand have been instrumental in keeping the tradition of Thai calligraphy alive and thriving in the modern age. These individuals and organizations, who are dedicated to preserving and promoting Thailand's rich cultural heritage, have worked tirelessly to ensure that the art form continues to evolve and inspire future generations.

One such individual is Ajarn Nai Saengchan, a renowned Thai calligrapher who has dedicated his life to teaching and promoting the art form. Through his workshops, exhibitions, and publications, Ajarn Nai Saengchan has helped to foster a greater appreciation for Thai calligraphy and its role in shaping Thailand's artistic identity.

Traditional Painting

The origins of traditional Thai painting can be traced back to ancient times, with the earliest known examples dating to the prehistoric period. The development of Thai painting has been shaped by numerous cultural influences, including those from India, China, and the Khmer Empire. As a result, Thai painting has evolved into a unique and sophisticated art form, characterized by its distinctive styles, techniques, and themes.

The timeline of traditional Thai painting can be broadly divided into several key periods, each marked by significant artistic developments and the emergence of distinct schools of painting. The earliest known paintings, dating back to the 7th century, were discovered in the ancient city of Dvaravati and exhibit strong Indian influences. The subsequent Khmer period, spanning the 9th to the 13th centuries, witnessed the infusion of Khmer artistic elements into Thai painting, resulting in a distinctive fusion of styles.

The Sukhothai period, from the 13th to the 15th centuries, is often regarded as the golden age of Thai art and culture. During this time, Thai painting flourished, with artists developing a unique and refined style characterized by graceful figures, delicate lines, and intricate detail. The Ayutthaya period, which followed the Sukhothai era, saw the continuation and further refinement of these artistic traditions, as well as the introduction of new techniques and motifs.

The Rattanakosin period, which began in the late 18th century and continues to the present day, has been marked by the emergence of several distinct schools of Thai painting. These schools, each with its characteristic style and techniques, include the Bangkok School, the Lanna School, and the Udon School, among others. Throughout this period, Thai painting has continued to evolve, incorporating new influences and adapting to changing cultural contexts while maintaining its distinctive identity.

Traditional Thai painting is characterized by its meticulous attention to detail, refined brushwork, and vibrant color palette. Artists employ a range of techniques to achieve these effects, including the use of fine brushes made from animal hair, intricate layering of colors, and the application of gold leaf for added luminosity.

The materials used in traditional Thai painting are as diverse as the techniques employed by its practitioners. Natural pigments derived from minerals, plants, and other organic sources form the basis of the color palette, while the use of gold leaf adds a touch of opulence and spiritual significance. The support for these paintings varies, with artists working on a range of surfaces, including cloth, paper, and wood.

Recurring themes and motifs in traditional Thai painting reflect the country's rich cultural heritage and the profound influence of Buddhism on its artistic traditions. Nature, mythology, and religious symbolism feature prominently in these works, with depictions of celestial beings, sacred animals, and idyllic landscapes serving as visual manifestations of the spiritual beliefs and values that underpin Thai society.

Throughout its history, traditional Thai painting has produced a pantheon of distinguished artists whose contributions have shaped the art form and elevated it to new heights of artistic expression. Among these luminaries are painters such as Khrua In Khong, a master craftsman, and painter who served at the court of King Rama III, and Chakrabhand Posayakrit, a renowned painter and scholar who played a pivotal role in the revival of Thai mural painting in the 20th century.

Significant works of traditional Thai painting can be found in temples, palaces, and museums throughout the country, bearing testament to the artistic prowess and cultural significance of this revered art form. Notable examples include the magnificent murals that adorn the walls of Wat Phra Kaew, the Temple of the Emerald Buddha, in Bangkok and the exquisite paintings that grace the interior of the Viharn Phra Mongkol Bophit at Ayutthaya's Wat Phra Si Sanphet.

The influence of traditional Thai painting extends beyond the borders of Thailand, with contemporary artists drawing inspiration from its rich artistic legacy and incorporating elements of its style and technique into their work. This enduring influence is a testament to the power of traditional Thai painting to captivate and inspire, transcending the boundaries of time and culture to speak to the universal human experience.

Pottery and Ceramics

Thailand, a land steeped in vibrant culture and ancient traditions, boasts a rich artistic heritage that extends far beyond its magnificent temples and intricate silk weavings. Among the many treasures that embody the essence of Thai artistry, pottery, and ceramics stand out as a testament to the nation's enduring creative spirit. From the delicate celadon wares of Sukhothai to the vibrant stoneware of Chiang Mai, Thai pottery has captivated collectors and connoisseurs for centuries, offering a glimpse into the soul of a nation.

Pottery, an art form as old as civilization itself, has played an integral role in Thai culture for millennia. Its significance transcends mere functionality, weaving itself into the fabric of daily life, religious practices, and artistic expression. In ancient times, pottery served as a vital tool for storing food and water, cooking, and performing rituals. Its versatility and durability made it an indispensable companion in the lives of ordinary people and royalty alike.

As Thai society evolved, so did the role of pottery. It became a canvas for expressing artistic vision, with skilled artisans crafting exquisite pieces that reflected the beauty and complexity of their world. The intricate designs, vibrant colors, and meticulous craftsmanship of Thai pottery elevated it from utilitarian objects to cherished works of art, admired for their aesthetic appeal and cultural significance.

The history of Thai pottery is a captivating tale of innovation, adaptation, and cultural exchange. Archaeological evidence suggests that pottery production in Thailand dates back to the Neolithic period, with simple earthenware vessels serving the basic needs of early communities. Over time, techniques and styles evolved, influenced by interactions with neighboring civilizations and the rise of powerful kingdoms.

The Sukhothai Kingdom (13th-15th centuries) marked a golden age for Thai pottery. Renowned for its celadon wares, characterized by their delicate green glaze and intricate floral motifs, Sukhothai pottery gained international acclaim and became a symbol of Thai artistic excellence. The influence of Chinese porcelain techniques is evident in the refinement and sophistication of Sukhothai ceramics, while the unique Thai aesthetic shines through in the graceful forms and intricate decorations.

Following the decline of Sukhothai, other regional styles emerged, each with its distinctive characteristics. Chiang Mai, in northern Thailand, became known for its vibrant stoneware, often adorned with bold colors and intricate designs inspired by local flora and fauna. In the south, the influence of Khmer ceramics is evident in the use of earthenware and the prevalence of religious motifs.

Throughout the centuries, Thai pottery has continued to evolve, reflecting changing social, economic, and cultural trends. The introduction of new technologies and materials has led to innovative forms and designs, while traditional techniques and styles are still cherished and preserved by skilled artisans.

The creation of Thai pottery is a mesmerizing blend of tradition and artistry. Skilled artisans employ a variety of techniques, each contributing to the unique character and beauty of the finished product. Hand-building, a time-honored method involving shaping clay by hand, is still widely practiced, particularly for creating intricate and delicate forms. Wheel throwing, a technique that involves shaping clay on a rotating wheel, allows for greater precision and symmetry in the creation of vessels and other objects.

Glazing, the application of a thin layer of glass-like material, adds a protective layer to pottery while enhancing its aesthetic appeal. Thai potters have mastered the art of glazing, producing a wide range of colors and textures that add depth and richness to their creations. From the translucent celadon glaze of Sukhothai to the vibrant cobalt blue of Chiang Mai, Thai glazes are an integral part of the pottery's identity.

The uses of Thai pottery in daily life are as diverse as the styles themselves. Storage containers, cooking vessels, and tableware are just a few examples of how pottery has served practical purposes in Thai households for generations. The durability and versatility of pottery have made it a reliable companion in the kitchen, while its aesthetic appeal has elevated it to a decorative art form, adorning homes and public spaces with elegance and charm.

In Thai culture, pottery transcends its utilitarian function to play a significant role in rituals and ceremonies. From ancient animistic beliefs to Buddhist practices, pottery has served as a sacred vessel, connecting the physical world with the spiritual realm.

In animistic traditions, pottery was believed to be imbued with spirits and used in offerings to appease deities and ancestors. The intricate designs and symbolic motifs found on many Thai pottery pieces reflect these beliefs, serving as a visual language that communicates with the unseen world.

Buddhist ceremonies also incorporate pottery, with monks using alms and bowls made of ceramic to collect offerings from the faithful. These bowls, often adorned with auspicious symbols and religious motifs, represent the virtue of humility and the importance of giving.

The use of pottery in rituals and ceremonies underscores its deep-rooted significance in Thai culture. It serves as a tangible expression of faith, tradition, and the interconnectedness of the physical and spiritual realms.

Thailand is home to numerous renowned pottery centers, each with its unique history, style, and traditions. These centers have played a pivotal role in shaping the evolution of Thai pottery, preserving ancient techniques while fostering innovation and creativity.

Sukhothai, the cradle of Thai celadon, remains a revered center for pottery production. The city's rich history is evident in the numerous kilns and workshops that continue to produce exquisite celadon wares, adhering to centuries-old techniques and designs. The delicate green glaze, intricate floral motifs, and graceful forms of Sukhothai pottery continue to captivate collectors and art enthusiasts worldwide.

Chiang Mai, nestled in the mountainous north, is another renowned pottery center. Its vibrant stoneware, characterized by bold colors, intricate designs, and influences from Lanna culture, has earned international recognition. Chiang Mai potters are celebrated for their mastery of glazes, producing a stunning array of colors and textures that add depth and richness to their creations.

Ratchaburi, located in the western region of Thailand, is renowned for its production of earthenware and stoneware. The province's rich clay deposits have fostered a thriving pottery industry, with artisans specializing in a wide range of styles and techniques. From traditional water jars to contemporary decorative pieces, Ratchaburi pottery reflects the region's cultural heritage and artistic diversity.

These centers of excellence, along with numerous smaller workshops scattered throughout the country, continue to preserve and promote the rich tradition of Thai pottery. They serve as hubs of creativity, where skilled artisans pass down their knowledge and techniques to younger generations, ensuring that the legacy of Thai pottery lives on for centuries to come.

Sculpture

Among the many treasures that embody the essence of Thai artistry, the sculpture stands out as a testament to the nation's profound reverence for the divine, its deep-rooted cultural beliefs, and its unwavering pursuit of aesthetic excellence. From the majestic bronze Buddhas of Sukhothai to the intricate wood carvings of Chiang Mai, Thai sculpture has captivated the world with its captivating beauty, profound symbolism, and enduring legacy.

Thailand's artistic heritage is deeply intertwined with its religious beliefs, with sculpture playing a pivotal role in expressing devotion, narrating sacred stories, and embodying the essence of the divine. The majority of Thai sculptures are inspired by Buddhism, the predominant religion in the country, reflecting the core tenets of compassion, enlightenment, and the pursuit of nirvana. Hindu influences are also evident in some sculptures, particularly those depicting deities and mythological figures from the Hindu pantheon.

The artistic heritage of Thailand is not merely confined to religious expression. Secular themes also find their place in Thai sculpture, with artists depicting scenes from everyday life, royal court ceremonies, and mythological tales. These sculptures offer valuable insights into the social, cultural, and political landscape of Thailand throughout history, providing a tangible record of the nation's evolving traditions and values.

The history of Thai sculpture is a captivating tale of innovation, adaptation, and cultural exchange. Archaeological evidence suggests that the art of sculpture in Thailand dates back to the prehistoric period, with simple terracotta figures serving as early examples of artistic expression. Over time, techniques and styles evolved, influenced by interactions with neighboring civilizations and the rise of powerful kingdoms.

The Dvaravati period (6th-11th centuries) marked the emergence of sophisticated stone sculptures, heavily influenced by Indian artistic traditions. These sculptures, often depicting Buddhist deities and scenes from the Jataka tales, showcased the mastery of Thai artisans in carving intricate details and conveying profound spiritual messages.

The Sukhothai Kingdom (13th-15th centuries) ushered in a golden age for Thai sculpture. Renowned for its bronze Buddhas, characterized by their serene expressions, graceful postures, and elongated earlobes, Sukhothai sculpture achieved a level of refinement and elegance that has captivated art enthusiasts for centuries. The influence of Theravada Buddhism is evident in the serene beauty and contemplative nature of Sukhothai sculptures, reflecting the pursuit of inner peace and enlightenment.

Following the decline of Sukhothai, other regional styles emerged, each with its distinctive characteristics. The Ayutthaya Kingdom (14th-18th centuries) saw the rise of monumental sculptures, often depicting larger-than-life Buddhas and elaborate temple decorations. The influence of Khmer art is evident in the grandeur and architectural integration of Ayutthaya sculptures, while the unique Thai aesthetic shines through in the intricate details and expressive forms.

The Rattanakosin period (18th century onwards) witnessed a revival of traditional styles and the introduction of new influences. European artistic trends, particularly those from the Renaissance and Baroque periods, found their way into Thai sculpture, resulting in a fusion of Eastern and Western aesthetics. This period also saw the rise of portraiture, with sculptures depicting members of the royal family and prominent figures in Thai society.

Throughout the centuries, Thai sculpture has continued to evolve, reflecting changing social, economic, and cultural trends. The introduction of new materials and technologies has led to innovative forms and designs, while traditional techniques and styles are still cherished and preserved by skilled artisans.

Thai sculptures are not merely aesthetic objects; they serve as sacred vessels, embodying the essence of the divine and connecting the physical world with the spiritual realm. In Buddhist temples, sculptures of the Buddha are revered as objects of worship, offering solace, inspiration, and a tangible connection to the enlightened being. The serene expressions, graceful postures, and intricate details of these sculptures invite contemplation and inspire devotion among followers.

Hindu deities, such as Brahma, Vishnu, and Shiva, are also depicted in Thai sculptures, reflecting the influence of Hinduism on Thai culture. These sculptures often adorn temple walls and shrines, serving as reminders of the divine presence and the interconnectedness of all things.

The religious significance of Thai sculptures extends beyond their role as objects of worship. They also serve as teaching tools, narrating sacred stories from Buddhist and Hindu scriptures. The intricate carvings and symbolic gestures of these sculptures convey complex theological concepts and moral lessons, making them accessible to a wider audience.

The creation of Thai sculptures is a mesmerizing blend of tradition and artistry. Skilled artisans employ a variety of materials and techniques, each contributing to the unique character and beauty of the finished product.

Bronze casting has been a revered technique in Thailand for centuries, particularly for creating large-scale sculptures of the Buddha. The intricate process involves creating a mold, pouring molten bronze into the mold, and meticulously refining the surface to achieve a smooth and lustrous finish. The bronze Buddhas of Sukhothai, with their serene expressions and graceful postures, stand as a testament to the mastery of Thai bronze casters.

Wood carving is another widely practiced technique in Thailand, particularly for creating smaller sculptures and decorative elements. Teakwood, known for its durability and intricate grain, is a popular choice for wood carving. Skilled artisans use a variety of tools and techniques to shape the wood, creating intricate details, expressive forms, and graceful curves. The intricate wood carvings of Chiang Mai, often depicting scenes from Buddhist mythology and everyday life, showcase the artistry of Thai woodcarvers.

Stone carving is also an important technique in Thai sculpture, particularly for creating monumental sculptures and architectural elements. Sandstone, granite, and marble are commonly used materials, offering durability and a canvas for intricate details. The stone sculptures of Ayutthaya, with their grandeur and architectural integration, demonstrate the mastery of Thai stone carvers.

Thailand is home to numerous iconic sculptures that have become symbols of the nation's artistic heritage and religious devotion. These sculptures captivate visitors with their beauty, profound symbolism, and enduring legacy.

The Emerald Buddha, enshrined in Wat Phra Kaew in Bangkok, is perhaps the most revered sculpture in Thailand. Carved from a single block of jade, the Emerald Buddha is believed to have been created in India in the 4th century and has a long and fascinating history. Its serene expression, graceful posture, and intricate details embody the essence of Theravada Buddhism and inspire awe and devotion among followers.

The Walking Buddha statue, located at Wat Arun in Bangkok, is another iconic sculpture that attracts visitors from around the world. This colossal statue, standing over 30 meters tall, depicts the Buddha in the act of taking a step forward, symbolizing his journey towards enlightenment and the impermanence of all things. The intricate details of the statue, including the elaborate patterns on the Buddha's robe and the serene expression on his face, make it a masterpiece of Thai sculpture.

Thai sculpture has had a profound impact on society and the arts, both within Thailand and beyond. Its influence can be seen in the architecture of temples, the design of everyday objects, and the development of other art forms, such as painting and literature.

Thai sculptures have served as a source of inspiration for artists and artisans for centuries, influencing the development of new styles and techniques. The serene beauty and graceful forms of Thai sculptures have also had a profound impact on the spiritual and cultural landscape of the nation, fostering a sense of reverence for the divine and promoting the values of compassion, enlightenment, and inner peace.

Beyond Thailand, Thai sculpture has gained international recognition and appreciation. Museums and private collections worldwide house masterpieces of Thai sculpture, showcasing the nation's artistic heritage and cultural significance. The intricate details, profound symbolism, and enduring beauty of Thai sculptures continue to captivate art enthusiasts and inspire creativity around the world.

The artistic traditions of Thailand have remained resilient and enduring despite evolving identities. Inspired by nature and mythology, Thai artwork reflects the interconnectedness of life cycles, embodying subtle beauty and patience through symbolism and narrative. Even as Thai art engages with globalization, it continues to honor the delicate balance between humanity and the environment.

Thai artistry celebrates regional diversity within a unified national style, and it remains a living tradition thanks to continued patronage. Modern issues are addressed through classical forms, and young artisans are adapting ancient crafts to ensure their preservation. Thailand's rich artistic heritage has also inspired global communities, with its foundations in animism, religion, and royal patronage laying the groundwork for enduring conventions of connection, storytelling, and technical brilliance.

By understanding these origins, one can gain insight into the timeless philosophies that underpin Thai art, ensuring its culturally-rooted self-expression will continue to evolve and flourish in the future.

Cultural Influences

Thailand's central location in mainland Southeast Asia, bordered by Myanmar, Laos, Cambodia, and Malaysia, has made it a natural crossroads for the movement of people, ideas, and artistic styles. Geographical proximity has facilitated trade and migration between the Thai kingdom and its neighbors, resulting in a dynamic exchange of cultural influences that has enriched Thai art.

The influence of Chinese art on Thai art is evident in the adoption of Chinese styles and motifs in painting, sculpture, and architecture from the Dvaravati era (6th-11th centuries CE) onwards. The introduction of Buddhism to Thailand from China brought with it a rich tradition of Buddhist iconography, which was absorbed and adapted by Thai artists to create a unique synthesis of Chinese and indigenous styles.

One notable example of Chinese influence is the integration of decorative techniques such as lacquerwork into Thai art. Lacquer, made from the sap of the lac tree, was imported from China and used to decorate a variety of objects, including furniture, religious artifacts, and architectural elements. Thai artists developed their distinctive styles of lacquerware, characterized by intricate designs and vibrant colors.

The introduction of Hindu and Buddhist philosophies from India had a profound impact on the development of Thai religious art. The adoption of sculptural styles such as Buddha poses and the architecture of South Indian temples can be seen in many Thai temples, such as Wat Phra Si Sanphet in Ayutthaya and Wat Arun in Bangkok.

Indian influence can also be seen in the use of stucco and plaster in the decoration of Thai temples. Stucco, a type of plaster made from lime, sand, and water, was used to create intricate relief sculptures and ornamental motifs. This technique was imported from India and adapted by Thai artists to create a unique style of temple decoration that combines Indian, Khmer, and indigenous Thai elements.

The political and cultural influence of the Khmer Empire in northern Thailand is evident in the borrowing of monumental architectural styles in Thai temples, such as the use of sandstone and laterite in temple construction, and the adaptation of Khmer carving and sculpture techniques into Thai styles. The Angkor Wat temple complex in Cambodia, built during the height of the Khmer Empire, is a prime example of the grandeur and sophistication of Khmer architecture, which had a lasting impact on Thai art and architecture.

Despite the many external influences on Thai art, Thai artists have been able to create a distinctive artistic idiom that reflects the country's unique Buddhist cosmology. This synthesis of multiple influences can be seen in the development of artistic traditions such as the creation of Buddha images, the decoration of temples, and the production of textiles.

Thai Buddha images, for example, are characterized by their serene facial expressions, elongated ears, and graceful poses, which reflect the Thai ideal of spiritual enlightenment. Thai temple decoration, meanwhile, combines ornate carvings, intricate stucco work, and vibrant colors to create a visual feast that reflects the richness and complexity of Thai Buddhist cosmology.

The growth of maritime trade routes along the Chao Phraya delta in the 14th century spurred economic growth and facilitated the exchange of artistic ideas and materials between Thailand and distant cultures. Contact with traders from China, India, the Middle East, and Europe introduced new art materials and styles, which were absorbed and adapted by Thai artists to create a unique hybrid artistic heritage.

The importation of materials such as glass, lacquer, and paper from China had a significant impact on Thai art. Glass beads, for example, were used to decorate textiles, while lacquer was used to create intricate designs on furniture and religious artifacts. Paper, which was imported from China and later produced locally, was used to create manuscripts, folding screens, and other decorative objects.

The integration of Islamic geometric motifs into Thai textiles is a notable example of cross-cultural influence. These motifs, which were introduced to Thailand through trade with the Middle East, were absorbed and adapted by Thai weavers to create a unique style of textile design that combines geometric patterns with floral and animal motifs.

Japanese Ukiyo-e prints, which became popular in Thailand in the 19th century, also had a significant impact on Thai art. These prints, which depicted scenes from everyday life, inspired Thai artists to create their genre of painting that focused on the daily lives of ordinary people. European techniques, such as the use of perspective and shading, were also blended with Thai painting styles to create a hybrid art form that combined traditional and modern elements.

Royal and merchant patronage played a crucial role in the development of Thai art. The Thai court was a major patron of the arts, commissioning works of art for religious and ceremonial purposes. Merchants, meanwhile, played an important role in the production and distribution of art, sponsoring the creation of works that reflected their wealth and status.

The export of Thai art also encouraged cultural exchanges with foreign countries. Thai art was highly prized by collectors in Europe and America, and the demand for Thai art helped to stimulate the development of new styles and techniques. The commercialization of Thai art, however, also had an impact on traditional art forms, as artists began to produce works that catered to the tastes of foreign buyers.

The dynamic interplay between local and foreign artistic traditions has been a consistent theme in the development of Thai art. The enduring legacy of cultural exchange can be seen in the continued evolution of uniquely Thai hybrid artistic heritage, which combines elements of Chinese, Indian, Khmer, and other cultural influences to create a distinctive artistic idiom that reflects the richness and complexity of Thai culture.

The artistic heritage of Thailand is a testament to the country's rich cultural history and its ability to absorb and adapt to external influences while maintaining its unique identity. The interplay between local and foreign artistic traditions has resulted in a dynamic and evolving artistic heritage that is a source of pride and inspiration for the Thai people. By understanding the historical and cultural contexts in which Thai art has developed, we can gain a deeper appreciation for the beauty and complexity of this rich artistic tradition.

Regional Variations

The Kingdom of Thailand is home to a rich of artistic traditions that have developed across its diverse regions, shaped profoundly by unique cultural influences. Nowhere is this artistic variety more apparent than in Northern Thailand, where the synthesis of Lanna and Burmese styles forged distinctive visual languages throughout centuries of cultural exchange. From woodcarving to sculpture and painting, the artistic heritage of Northern Thailand stands as a celebration of cross-cultural assimilation and the enduring spirit of local craftsmanship.

Situated along historic trade routes connecting Thailand with its neighbors to the west and north, the ancient Lanna Kingdom, centered around present-day Chiang Mai and Lamphun, incorporated aspects of Burmese and Mon artistic traditions that distinctly informed Northern Thai art forms. Under the Lanna royal court from the 13th to 16th centuries, Buddhist and secular art flourished as skilled artisans fused technical know-how from various cultural spheres into woodcarving, architecture, lacquerware, and other visual arts. This syncretism of stylistic influences established signatures native to the region that have since become celebrated hallmarks of Northern Thai artistic legacy.

With the growth of commerce between Lanna and its northern neighbors via the Chao Phraya River system, Burmese lacquerware, and woodcarving techniques found fertile artistic exchange. Guilds of craftspeople in Chiang Mai and surrounding towns mastered a distinctive wood gilding style incorporating gold leaf and inlaid mother-of-pearl, developing ornate styles for Buddhist temple architecture and religious iconography. Similarly, the techniques of working lacquer into elegantly designed household items and containers fused Lanna and Burmese technical sensibilities. Through a dynamic yet organic process of adaptation, emulation, and localized innovation over centuries, these cultural confluences formulated seminal Northern Thai art forms with Lanna identity at their core.

Woodcarving: Renowned as a preeminent Lanna art, intricate woodcarving flourished under royal patronage and Buddhist auspices. Temple architecture showcases grand gilded Woodcarvings depicting Jataka tales and enlightened imagery. Skilled carvers produced religious statuary, furniture, and intricate household items embellished with gold leaf, mother-of-pearl, and stylized motifs reflecting the assimilation of Burmese and Mon styles into a distinctly Northern signature.

Lacquerware: One of Thailand's most sophisticated art forms, Northern Thai lacquerware fused Burmese techniques with original Lanna designs of carved and painted scenes and patterns. Intricately inlaid and multi-colored, lacquerware found applications from betel nut sets and containers to decorative household accessories and furnishings. Renowned for durability and exquisite craftsmanship, lacquerware became a prized artisanal export.

Terracotta Sculpture: Centered in the twin traditions of Phrae and Lampang, clay sculpture emerged as a celebrated Northern Thai art. Depicting Buddhist, secular, and mythical themes, terracotta pieces ranged from small ornamental artifacts to lifesize temple statuary and architectural embellishments, often festooned with colorful glazes. This tradition, though less renowned today, defined an entire visual culture.

Bronze Casting: Historically concentrated in Phrae and Lampang-like terracotta sculpture, bronze casting produced elaborately detailed religious icons in the Buddhist tradition. Skilled artisans crafted fine anatomical features and ornate costumes worthy of royal temples. Both lost wax and piece-mold techniques yielded freestanding statues and relief artwork of considerable technical prowess.

The 20th century marked a renaissance in Northern Thai arts through major figures who stewarded traditional techniques while embracing modern expressions.

Silpa Bhirasri: Founding father of modern Thai art, this Italian-Thai artist directed Chiang Mai University's prestigious fine arts school in the 1930s. Emphasizing academic approaches and heritage appreciation, his initiative reinvigorated woodcarving, lacquerware, and other mediums by elite disciples who developed styles integrating regional flair.

Thawan Duchanee: A National Artist acknowledged for pioneering modern Lanna painting styles-infusing folkloric and Buddhist themes with abstract experimentation. Displaying at Bangkok's Silpakorn University, his vibrant compositions helped elevate local arts into the national limelight.

Ninin Eamsa-ard: From Phrae, this renowned sculptor crafted monumental religious works in terracotta and bronze while successfully transplanting indigenous styles into contemporary sculptures-commenting on Buddhist and social themes shown internationally.

Chalermchai Kositpipat: A multi-disciplinary artist from Lampang, his wood reliefs, lacquerware, and paintings balance tradition and progression. His lively Jataka murals adorn temples, while modern takes on folktales are exhibited globally. As director of the National Gallery's Northern Art Museum, he fosters new generations of artists.

Various initiatives celebrate and sustain Northern Thai artistic legacy. Major monuments like Chiang Mai's historic temples house invaluable woodcarvings, lacquerware, and sculptures. Museums specializing in regional arts include the National Gallery's Northern Art Museum in Lampang and Chiang Mai's Fine Arts Museum. Conservation efforts focus on safeguarding endangered traditions and training younger artisans. Revival programs have bolstered lacquerware and woodcarving production centered in Chiang Mai. Such endeavors help ensure Northern Thailand's vibrant arts remain dynamic and accessible to new generations of Thais and the world.

Central Thailand rose as a cultural fulcrum, harnessing artistic skills from surrounding regions into exquisite Siamese styles. Under royal Siamese courts based in Ayutthaya and later Bangkok, Central Thai visual arts were catalyzed to epitomize national identity and cosmopolitan Siam's links with neighbors. Despite modern societal changes, Central Thai artistic expression remains society's intuitive soul.

During Ayutthaya's ascendancy (14th-18th centuries) as a dominant trading kingdom, Central Thai culture flourished with royal sponsorship nurturing temple architecture, sculpture, and painterly traditions. Buddhist and Brahmanic influences shaped artistic media from wood to stucco as skilled craftsmen materialized stories of faith. When Burmese invaders sacked Ayutthaya in 1767, Bangkok arose as Rattanakosin—a resilient cultural heart enabling royal premieres like King Rama I and III to revive artistic glory through temple works. Renaissance occurred under King Mongkut and skilled artisans, with King Chulalongkorn's reign commencing modern development in the arts.

Painting: Preshowcasing tales of religion and the kingdom's glory, mural, and scroll paintings ornamented temple interiors and palaces in vividly emotive styles. Elite court painters documented landscapes and portraits with care and passion.

Sculpture: Exquisite stucco, terracotta, and bronze icons of Buddha, Hindu deities, and auspicious figures embellished Ayutthaya and Bangkok architectures with anatomical accuracy and fine ornamentation.

Architecture: Graceful prang towers, vaulted roofs and ornamental facades of Central Thai temples embodied refined amalgamations of indigenous, Hindu-Buddhist, and later European influences in awe-inspiring constructions.

Textiles: Central Thailand was renowned for intricately patterned silk and cotton textiles for royalty, temples, and people. Elegant weaving and embroidery traditions endured, diversifying techniques to become modern industry.

Dedicated royal patronage and temple sponsorship ensured artistic traditions' longevity until modern changes. Mass printing and photography impacted court painting while nationalism motivated artistic modernism. During post-war industrial growth, cottage crafts faced challenges yet dynamic young artists integrated techniques innovatively with social commentary. Revival initiatives helped safeguard textile, lacquer, and other crafts facing obsolescence, as visionary artists and cultural preservationists recognized heritage's role in fostering national identity and connections to humanity's rich wellspring of skill and imagination.

Central Thailand nourishes artistic continuity through heritage sites, temples, institutes, and international collaborations. National Museums in Bangkok house collections spanning history. Silpakorn, Chulalongkorn and King Mongkut universities nurture artistic traditions through teaching and research. Projects revitalize communities by helping artisans access wider markets. National identity is thus consciously cultivated while celebrating diversity through exchanges illuminating our shared well of creativity. Enduring artistic legacy ensures Siamese culture's soul resonates intrinsically in postmodern times, empowering societies everywhere to actualize both continuity and progression.

Southern Thailand's visual culture emerged from a dynamic convergence of foreign influences upon a rich indigenous fabric. Across centuries, the region incubated a vivid tapestry of artistic threads that distinguish Southern expression as a vibrant reflection of her people's diversity. Though contemporary shifts impact traditions, communities uphold this heritage by weaving continuity into new generations.

Southern Thailand's accessible shores invited the permeation of foreign aesthetics – especially from Malay, Chinese, and Indian civilizations who traded through her ports.

Textiles absorbed dyes, patterns, and techniques from abroad, incorporating local plant motifs into vibrantly patterned songket, prai, and fabric arts. Simultaneously, these external stimulations fortified the expression of a proud Southern Thai identity through selective cultural synthesis. The region became a lively conduit where global currents blended upon local shores to yield novel artistic styles.

Shadow Puppetry: Nakhon Si Thammarat preserved Thailand's most intricate leather puppet tradition depicting folklore and religious teachings through articulated shadow-play. Regional variants emerged with vibrantly painted characters and musical styles.

Sculpture: Vivid terracotta figures and architectural stucco embellished regional religious sites, adapting Indian and Srivijayan influences to the vernacular tropical aesthetic.

Textiles: Brilliantly dyed songket, patterned pha-kin, and delicate mats showcase the diverse ethnic threads interwoven across the southern tapestry - whether Malays, Chinese, Muslims, or indigenous groups.

Architecture: Southern Thai temples and mosques reflected each community's unique adaptation of architectural styles to the lush environment through colorful painting, woodcarving, and structural designs.

Distinct artistic signatures emerged across Southern provinces due to historical settlements and trade links. Nakhon Si Thammarat, Phatthalung, and Songkhla inherited strong Malay accents. Trang and Satun harbored unique Chinese and indigenous Bunong threads. Pattani, Yala, and Narathiwat mirrored their Muslim communities' unique religious artistic expressions through architecture, decoration, and crafts like silverwork. Regional folk art, textile patterning, and musical and performing art traditions showcase Southern Thailand's picturesque cultural mosaic.

Grassroots initiatives revitalize traditions through training younger generations of artisans and performers. Community museums and cultural centers share this diversity regionally and globally. Shadow puppet and folk performance groups attract new enthusiasts. Weaving co-ops help sustain livelihoods and living traditions. Government support facilitates artistic research and preservation, recognizing the heritage's role in fostering localized identities and regional pride across Thailand's rich cultural palette. Through such continuity, Southern Thailand's varied artistic strands will long enrich the nation's diverse tapestry.

Northeastern Thailand incubated prolific artistic traditions that infuse the region's soul. Though industrial changes impact age-old crafts, communities preserve this heritage bypassing life's beauty and spiritual nourishment to new generations. Isaan arts thus remain dynamic echoes of a people deeply tied to their landscape and Lao cultural ancestry.

Historically, the Lao kingdom saw intense cultural exchange with what is now Isaan. Sculptural styles like Sikhottabong terracotta figures shaped religious art. Performing traditions like likely spoken drama, maw lam long-form song, and pha biang shadow puppetry proliferated at temples and ceremonies. Farming communities cherished folk musical styles and poetry as vivid oral archives. Through adaptive assimilation, such influences imbued Northeast Thailand's artistic identity with an intrinsic Lao character.

Woodcarving: Ornate designs for wat architecture and furniture flourished around Khon Kaen and Kalasin, integrating Lao, central Thai, and Indigenous stylistic threads.

Ceramics: Terracotta figures, statuary, and containers featured in Buddhist and secular contexts center on Khon Kaen, blending function with exquisite detailing.

Shadow Puppets: Pha biang tradition most vibrant in Ubon Ratchathani and Si Sa Ket depicted folkloric, moral, and religious stories through two-dimensional leather figures.

Textiles: Vibrant indigo patterned saa and delicate mats were crafted throughout alongside unique embroidery styles and headdresses.

Folk Performing Arts: Deeply infused ceremonies and festivals with poetic soul across the rice-farming calendar.

Isaan arts mirrored intrinsic connections between agrarian communities and the landscape since prehistory. Visual forms were a means of passing teachings, values, and history through generations as livelihoods changed. Regional variations evolved through the assimilation of outside influences yet Lao cultural ancestry remained resonant. Traditional and contemporary artists ensured this rich heritage maintains relevance as a dynamic vessel of Northeastern identity.

Community artists and groups perpetuate crafts, performances, and oral traditions handed down through families. Appreciation societies and museums archive and showcase intangible cultural heritage. Workshops initiate younger generations into carving, puppetry, music, and textile techniques. Festivals and competitions foster arts' visibility and prestige. Cooperative markets help artisans access sustainable livelihoods. Through such adaptive stewardship, Isaan's indigenous echoes will continue resonating into an unforeseeable future.

Through continuity and expression, Isaan's artistic legacy endures as a profound cultural carrier of Northeastern identity, ancestry, and landscape deeply tied to its ecology and communities.

While national styles unite Thailand's artistic heritage, regional variations reflect Thailand's cultural diversity. Distinct from centralized artistic canons, localized expressions evolved through geography, trade, and ethnic influences, fostering innovation within tradition. Though globalized, communities preserve indigenous identities through cultural stewardship. Comprehending Thailand's regional diversity provides nuanced insight into artistic foundations nurturing creativity nationwide. While styles blended through Thailand's dynamic history, regional artistry preserves diversity within national identity.

Community-driven expression sustains cultural sovereignty against global homogeneity. Comprehending Thailand's localized creativity provides nuanced insight into the richness, adaptability, and living connections of artistic heritage to landscapes, livelihoods, and ethnic roots across the nation.

Contemporary Thai Art

Thai art has a rich and diverse heritage that stretches back thousands of years. However, in the 20th century, the art scene in Thailand underwent significant changes as a result of modernization and exposure to Western art movements. In the early 20th century, Thai artists were exposed to Western art movements such as Impressionism and Art Nouveau. These movements had a profound impact on the development of modern Thai art, as artists began to experiment with new techniques and styles. Impressionism, with its emphasis on light, color, and atmosphere, influenced Thai artists to explore new ways of representing the natural world. Art Nouveau, with its flowing lines and organic forms, inspired Thai artists to create works that combined traditional motifs with modern aesthetics.

As Thai artists became more familiar with Western art movements, they also began to adopt modern techniques and materials. Perspective, which had not been a feature of traditional Thai art, began to be used to create a sense of depth and space in paintings. Oil paints, which were more versatile and vibrant than traditional materials, became popular among Thai artists. Photography, which had been introduced to Thailand in the late 19th century, also became an important medium for Thai artists.

The fusion of traditional and modern styles is a hallmark of contemporary Thai art. Silpa Bhirasri, an Italian artist and sculptor who founded the Fine Arts Department in Bangkok in 1933, played a significant role in promoting this fusion. Bhirasri encouraged Thai artists to integrate traditional motifs and techniques with modern styles and materials. This approach resulted in a unique blend of old and new that has come to define contemporary Thai art.

Contemporary Thai artists continue to blend traditional and modern styles in innovative ways. For example, some artists use traditional Thai motifs such as lotus flowers and nagas (mythical serpents) in their work, but reinterpret them using modern techniques and materials. Others combine traditional Thai art forms such as woodcarving and lacquerware with contemporary materials such as plastic and metal.

The exposure to Western art movements and the assimilation of modern techniques have had a lasting impact on contemporary Thai art. These developments have nurtured new expressions of Thai identity and enabled Thai artists to engage with the global art community on their terms. The fusion of traditional and modern styles has created a unique and dynamic art scene in Thailand that is constantly evolving and adapting to new influences.

Contemporary Thai art is a rich and complex tapestry that reflects the country's rich cultural heritage and its engagement with the modern world. The exposure to Western art movements and the assimilation of modern techniques have enabled Thai artists to create works that are both innovative and rooted in tradition. The fusion of traditional and modern styles has resulted in a unique and dynamic art scene that is constantly evolving and adapting to new influences. By recognizing and celebrating the rich cultural heritage of contemporary Thai art, we can gain a deeper appreciation for the beauty and complexity of this unique art form.

It is important to note that contemporary Thai art is not a monolithic entity, but rather a diverse and multifaceted field that encompasses a wide range of styles, techniques, and perspectives. From painting and sculpture to performance art and digital media, contemporary Thai artists are pushing the boundaries of what is possible and challenging traditional notions of art and culture. As such, contemporary Thai art is a vital and exciting field that offers a window into the rich cultural heritage of Thailand and its engagement with the modern world.

Some notable contemporary Thai artists include Rirkrit Tiravanija, who is known for his installations and performances that explore the intersection of art and everyday life;

Montien Boonma, who creates sculptures and installations that draw on traditional Thai motifs and materials; and Navin Rawanchaikul, who uses painting, installation, and performance to explore issues of identity, migration, and globalization. These artists, along with many others, are helping to shape the future of contemporary Thai art and ensure that it continues to evolve and thrive.

Contemporary Music

The contemporary Thai music scene is a rich tapestry of sounds and styles that reflect the country's complex cultural heritage and its engagement with the modern world. From traditional roots to new genres and global influences, contemporary Thai music is a vibrant and evolving field that offers a window into the rich cultural heritage of Thailand.

Thai music has a long and rich history, dating back thousands of years to the music of the ancient Khmer and Mon kingdoms. Traditional Thai music is characterized by its use of instruments such as the ranat (a type of xylophone), the khim (a type of dulcimer), and the pi (a type of flute). These instruments are often used in ensemble music, which is performed at religious ceremonies, royal functions, and other important events.

In the 20th century, traditional Thai music began to evolve as a result of exposure to Western music and instruments. The introduction of Western instruments such as the guitar, piano, and drums, as well as new genres such as pop and rock, had a profound impact on the development of contemporary Thai music. Thai musicians began to incorporate these new sounds and styles into their music, resulting in a unique fusion of traditional and modern elements.

The emergence of new genres is a hallmark of contemporary Thai music. Two of the most popular genres are mor lam and luk thung. Mor lam is a type of folk music that originated in the northeastern region of Thailand. It is characterized by its use of instruments such as the khaen (a type of bamboo mouth organ) and the phin (a type of lute). Mor lam songs often tell stories of rural life, love, and heartbreak.

Luk thung, on the other hand, is a type of country music that emerged in central Thailand in the mid-20th century. It is characterized by its use of Western instruments such as the guitar and drums, as well as its themes of rural life, social issues, and working-class struggles. Luk thung has become one of the most popular genres in Thailand, with many of its stars achieving national fame and fortune.

In recent years, the indie and alternative scenes have also emerged as important forces in contemporary Thai music. These scenes are characterized by their DIY ethos, experimentation with new sounds and styles, and engagement with social and political issues. Many indie and alternative artists are using social media and other digital platforms to reach new audiences and build a following both in Thailand and abroad.

Influences from abroad have also played an important role in shaping contemporary Thai music. K-pop, the popular music genre from South Korea, has had a particularly strong impact on Thai music. Many Thai artists have been inspired by K-pop's catchy melodies, slick production values, and high-energy performances. Some Thai artists have even collaborated with K-pop stars, resulting in chart-topping hits and increased exposure for both artists.

International styles such as hip-hop, R&B, and electronic dance music (EDM) have also influenced contemporary Thai music. Thai hip-hop artists such as Thaitanium and Joey Boy have achieved international success, while EDM festivals such as Wonderfruit and Waterzonic have become major events on the global music calendar.

Cultural exchange is an important aspect of contemporary Thai music. Festivals, concerts, and other events provide opportunities for artists to share their music with new audiences and collaborate with other musicians. Social media has also played a crucial role in expanding the global reach of Thai music. Artists can use platforms such as YouTube, Facebook, and Instagram to connect with fans around the world and share their work with a global audience.

Contemporary Thai music is a rich and diverse field that reflects the country's complex cultural heritage and its engagement with the modern world. From traditional roots to new genres and global influences, contemporary Thai music is a vibrant and evolving field that offers a window into the rich cultural heritage of Thailand. Whether through traditional instruments or modern sounds, Thai musicians are pushing the boundaries of what is possible and challenging traditional notions of music and culture. By recognizing and celebrating the diversity and complexity of contemporary Thai music, we can gain a deeper appreciation for the beauty and richness of this unique art form.

It is worth noting that contemporary Thai music is not without its challenges. Issues such as piracy, censorship, and lack of funding and support can make it difficult for artists to create and distribute their work. However, despite these challenges, contemporary Thai music continues to thrive and evolve, thanks to the passion and creativity of its artists and the support of its fans. As the world becomes increasingly interconnected, contemporary Thai music is sure to continue to play an important role in the global music scene, reflecting the rich cultural heritage of Thailand and its engagement with the modern world.

Modern Calligraphy

Thai calligraphy and typography have a long and rich history, dating back to the Sukhothai period in the 13th century. Traditional Thai scripts are characterized by their intricate and elegant designs, which are often used in religious and ceremonial contexts. In recent years, however, contemporary Thai calligraphy and typography have emerged as important fields that blend tradition with modernity, reflecting the cultural heritage of Thailand while also embracing new forms and applications.

One of the most significant developments in contemporary Thai calligraphy and typography has been the simplification of traditional scripts for use in print, advertising, and signage. Traditional Thai scripts are complex and time-consuming to write, making them impractical for use in modern contexts. As a result, simplified scripts have been developed that retain the beauty and elegance of traditional scripts while also being easier to read and write.

One example of this trend is the development of the Thai Sans font, which was created in the 1930s by Prince Narisara Nuwattiwong. Thai Sans is a simplified script that is based on traditional Thai scripts but has been modernized for use in print and digital media. It has become a popular font for use in advertising, signage, and packaging, as well as in websites and digital media.

Contemporary Thai calligraphy and typography have also given rise to new art forms that blend traditional and modern elements. Typography, for example, is increasingly being used in graphic design, murals, and tattoos. Thai typography is characterized by its use of intricate designs and patterns, which are often combined with modern typography techniques to create unique and eye-catching designs.

Murals and street art are also becoming popular forms of contemporary Thai calligraphy and typography. These works often incorporate traditional Thai motifs and scripts but are executed in a modern style that reflects the cultural heritage of Thailand while also embracing new forms and techniques. Tattoos are another form of contemporary Thai calligraphy and typography that have gained popularity in recent years. Traditional Thai tattoos, known as Sak Yant, are often done in a calligraphic style and are believed to have protective powers. Today, many people are getting modern Thai tattoos that incorporate traditional scripts and motifs in a contemporary style.

Contemporary Thai calligraphy and typography have a wide range of applications in modern contexts. Packaging, publishing, digital media, and websites are just a few examples of the fields that are making use of contemporary Thai calligraphy and typography.

Packaging is an area where contemporary Thai calligraphy and typography are particularly prominent. Many Thai products, such as food, cosmetics, and textiles, are exported around the world, and packaging is an important way to communicate the cultural heritage and quality of these products. Contemporary Thai calligraphy and typography are often used to create packaging that is both visually appealing and culturally resonant.

Publishing is another field where contemporary Thai calligraphy and typography are being used to great effect. Thai publishers are increasingly using contemporary Thai calligraphy and typography to create books that are both beautiful and functional. This is particularly true in the case of children's books, where contemporary Thai calligraphy and typography can be used to create engaging and educational texts that are also visually appealing.

Digital media and websites are also making use of contemporary Thai calligraphy and typography. Thai websites and digital media often incorporate traditional Thai scripts and motifs but use contemporary typography techniques to create designs that are both modern and culturally resonant.

While contemporary Thai calligraphy and typography are embracing new forms and applications, it is important to preserve the cultural heritage of traditional Thai scripts. Many traditional Thai scripts are at risk of being lost, as they are no longer taught in schools and are not widely used in modern contexts.

Efforts are being made to preserve the cultural heritage of traditional Thai scripts, however. Organizations such as the Thai Script and Typography Research and Development Centre are working to promote the study and preservation of traditional Thai scripts. They are also working to develop new technologies that can be used to teach and preserve traditional Thai scripts, such as digital fonts and interactive learning tools.

Contemporary Thai calligraphy and typography are important fields that blend tradition with modernity, reflecting the cultural heritage of Thailand while also embracing new forms and applications. From simplified scripts for print and advertising to new art forms such as murals and tattoos, contemporary Thai calligraphy and typography are making a significant impact on modern culture. While it is important to preserve the cultural heritage of traditional Thai scripts, contemporary Thai calligraphy and typography offer exciting new possibilities for the future of Thai art and design.

Painting and Visual Arts

Contemporary Thai painting and visual arts have undergone significant transformations in recent decades, reflecting the country's rapid modernization and increasing globalization. Thai artists are exploring new media, styles, and themes, while also drawing on traditional techniques and cultural heritage.

Chalermchai Kositpipat is one of the most well-known contemporary Thai painters, whose work has been exhibited internationally. His paintings are characterized by their vivid colors, intricate details, and surreal imagery. Kositpipat draws inspiration from Buddhist philosophy, Thai folklore, and contemporary social issues. His most famous work, the White Temple in Chiang Rai, is a stunning example of his unique style, combining traditional Thai architecture with modern art.

Vorapol Lerdsuwanarun is another prominent contemporary Thai painter, whose work explores the relationship between the human experience and the natural world. His paintings often feature landscapes and figures that are abstracted and distorted, creating a sense of mystery and ambiguity. Lerdsuwanarun's use of color and brushwork is highly expressive, conveying a wide range of emotions and moods.

Contemporary Thai painting and visual arts encompass a wide range of themes and trends, reflecting the diverse perspectives and experiences of Thai artists. Social commentary is a common theme, with many artists using their work to critique contemporary society and address pressing issues such as inequality, environmental degradation, and political corruption.

Abstract expressionism is another popular trend in contemporary Thai painting, as artists explore the expressive potential of color, form, and texture. Pop art is also gaining popularity, as artists incorporate elements of popular culture, such as comics, advertising, and consumer products, into their work.

In addition to traditional painting and sculpture, contemporary Thai artists are exploring new media, such as installations, performance art, and digital/video works. Installation art, in particular, has become a popular medium, as artists create immersive environments that engage the viewer's senses and challenge their perceptions. Performance art is also gaining popularity, as artists use their bodies and actions to explore social and political issues.

Digital and video art are also becoming more prominent, as artists use new technologies to create works that are interactive, dynamic, and responsive. These works often incorporate elements of traditional Thai art, such as calligraphy and textiles, while also exploring new forms and possibilities.

Contemporary Thai painting and visual arts are also being influenced by global trends and exchanges. Many Thai artists are studying abroad, and are exposed to new ideas, techniques, and perspectives. This has led to a blending of Eastern and Western styles, as artists draw on both traditional Thai art and contemporary international art.

This exchange is also evident in the increasing number of international art exhibitions and collaborations taking place in Thailand. For example, the Bangkok Art Biennale, which takes place every two years, showcases works by artists from around the world, while also highlighting the work of Thai artists. These events provide opportunities for cultural exchange and dialogue and help to promote the work of Thai artists on the international stage.

Modern Pottery and Ceramics

Thailand is renowned for its rich ceramic heritage, dating back thousands of years to the ancient civilizations of Ban Chiang and Sukhothai. Today, contemporary Thai ceramics continue to evolve, incorporating new techniques and aesthetics, while also maintaining a connection to the country's cultural history.

Traditional Thai ceramics were often produced using hand-building or wheel-throwing techniques, fired in wood-burning kilns, and decorated with intricate glazes and designs. In recent years, however, many contemporary ceramicists have begun to incorporate industrial methods, such as slip-casting and electric kilns, to create larger, more complex forms. This has allowed for the production of functional and decorative ceramics on a larger scale, while still maintaining the handmade quality that is so highly valued in Thai ceramics.

In addition to new production methods, contemporary Thai ceramicists are also experimenting with new glazing styles, such as raku and crystalline glazes, which create unique textures and patterns. These techniques, combined with traditional Thai glazes, such as celadon and temmoku, create a striking blend of old and new, reflecting the evolution of Thai ceramics.

Thawan Duchanee is one of the most well-known contemporary Thai ceramicists, whose work has been exhibited internationally. Duchanee draws on traditional Thai motifs and techniques, such as celadon glazes and figurative sculptures, but incorporates his unique style and vision. His works are known for their bold colors, intricate details, and surreal imagery, often depicting mythical creatures and spiritual themes.

Teresita Fernandez, a Thai-American ceramicist, is another notable contemporary ceramicist who blends traditional Thai techniques with modern aesthetics. Her works often feature minimalist forms and abstract patterns, inspired by her travels and experiences growing up in Thailand. Fernandez's ceramics are known for their elegant simplicity and understated beauty, reflecting the changing role of ceramics in contemporary society.

Contemporary Thai ceramics are also characterized by a departure from traditional forms and functions, with many artists exploring abstract and minimalist aesthetics. These works often depart from the ceremonial and functional ware that has traditionally been associated with Thai ceramics, instead focusing on the expressive potential of clay and glaze.

Abstract forms, such as those created by artist Rirkrit Tiravanija, are becoming increasingly popular, as they challenge traditional notions of beauty and functionality. Tiravanija's works often feature irregular shapes and surfaces, created through experimental glazing techniques, and are meant to provoke thought and reflection.

Minimalist ceramics, such as those created by artist Somluk Pantiboon, are also gaining popularity, as they emphasize the simplicity and purity of form. Pantiboon's works often feature clean lines, smooth surfaces, and a limited color palette, creating a sense of calm and serenity.

Ceramics have long been an important part of Thai culture, reflecting the country's history, beliefs, and social roles. Today, contemporary Thai ceramics continue to hold cultural significance, reflecting changing social roles and identities.

For example, many contemporary ceramicists are using their work to address social and environmental issues, such as consumerism, pollution, and gender roles. These works often incorporate found objects and unconventional materials, challenging traditional notions of what constitutes a ceramic object.

In addition, contemporary Thai ceramics are also being used to preserve and promote traditional Thai crafts and techniques. Many ceramicists are working to revive traditional glazes and techniques, such as celadon and temmoku, to preserve this important cultural heritage.

Sculpture and Installations

Contemporary Thai sculptors are reimagining traditional motifs and forms through new lenses, using materials such as metal, glass, and resin to create works that are both familiar and innovative. For example, artist Thasnai Sethaseree uses recycled materials such as newspaper and cardboard to create intricate sculptures that reference traditional Thai architecture and crafts. Similarly, artist Araya Rasdjarmrearnsook creates sculptures and installations that explore the intersection of traditional Thai culture and contemporary society, often incorporating elements of Buddhist philosophy and mythology.

There are many prominent contemporary Thai sculptors whose works are gaining international recognition. One such artist is Askew Nakpil, whose monumental sculptures often reference traditional Thai motifs and mythology. For example, his work "Naga" is a massive steel sculpture in the shape of a mythical Thai serpent, while his work "Garuda" is a bronze sculpture of the mythical bird-like creature that is often associated with the Thai monarchy.

Another prominent contemporary Thai sculptor is Natee Utarit, whose figurative sculptures often explore themes of identity, memory, and social commentary. For example, his work "The Realism of Dreams" features a series of life-sized sculptures of figures in various poses, each with a different expression or gesture. Utarit's works often incorporate elements of traditional Thai art, such as gold leaf and intricate carving, to create a sense of contrast and tension.

Installations and site-specific art are becoming increasingly popular in contemporary Thai sculpture and installations, as artists seek to create works that are responsive to their surroundings and engage with the viewer in new ways. For example, artist Rirkrit Tiravanija creates installations that often incorporate food and cooking, inviting viewers to participate in the creation and consumption of the work. Tiravanija's installations often reference traditional Thai culture and social practices, such as communal eating and the importance of hospitality.

Site-specific art is also gaining popularity in contemporary Thai sculpture and installations, as artists create works that are specifically designed for a particular location or context. For example, artist Nipan Oranniwesna creates installations and sculptures that are inspired by the natural environment and the materials that are found in it. Oranniwesna's works often incorporate elements of performance and ephemeral materials, such as leaves and flowers, to create a sense of impermanence and change.

Contemporary Thai sculpture and installations are also being influenced by global trends and themes, as artists engage with issues such as environmentalism, social justice, and human rights. For example, artist Pratchaya Phinthong creates installations and sculptures that explore the intersection of global trade and environmentalism, often using recycled or found materials to create works that are both beautiful and thought-provoking.

Geometric abstraction is another popular trend in contemporary Thai sculpture and installations, as artists explore the expressive potential of form and color. For example, artist Pinaree Sanpitak creates sculptures and installations that are inspired by the female form and the natural world, often incorporating geometric shapes and patterns to create a sense of harmony and balance.

Environmental art is also gaining popularity in contemporary Thai sculpture and installations, as artists seek to create works that are responsive to the natural environment and raise awareness about environmental issues. For example, artist Tawatchai Puntusawasdi creates installations and sculptures that are made from natural materials, such as bamboo and leaves, and are designed to change over time as they interact with the elements.

Social commentary is another important theme in contemporary Thai sculpture and installations, as artists use their work to address issues such as inequality, corruption, and political unrest. For example, artist Jakkai Siributr creates textile-based installations and sculptures that critique contemporary Thai society and politics, often incorporating traditional Thai motifs and materials to create a sense of irony and contrast.

Digital and Multimedia Art

One of the most significant developments in contemporary Thai art has been the emergence of new forms of digital and multimedia art. Digital photography, for example, has become an increasingly popular medium for Thai artists, allowing them to create images that are both visually stunning and conceptually challenging. Artists like

Manit Sriwanichpoom and Michael Shaowanasai are using digital photography to explore issues of identity, culture, and politics in new and innovative ways.

Net art, or art that is created specifically for the internet, is another form of digital and multimedia art that is gaining popularity in Thailand. Artists like Waroot Tepchaiya and Chaiyoot Pawaiyapruek are using the internet as a platform to create works that are interactive, participatory, and engaging. These works often explore issues of technology, communication, and social media in ways that are both thought-provoking and humorous.

Virtual and augmented reality are also becoming increasingly important in contemporary Thai art. These new technologies are allowing artists to create immersive, interactive experiences that transport viewers to new worlds and realities. Artists like Thasnai Sethaseree and Prapat Jiwarangsan are using virtual and augmented reality to explore issues of memory, identity, and spirituality in new and innovative ways.

Many artists and pioneers are leading the way in contemporary Thai digital and multimedia art. Waroot Tepchaiya, for example, is a technologist and artist who is known for his innovative use of technology in his work. Tepchaiya's work often explores issues of identity, culture, and technology, and he has created several interactive installations and performances that push the boundaries of what is possible in digital art.

Chaiyoot Pawaiyapruek is another pioneer in contemporary Thai digital and multimedia art. Pawaiyapruek is a multimedia artist and designer who has worked on a wide range of projects, from interactive installations to virtual reality experiences. His work often explores issues of technology, communication, and social media, and he is known for his ability to create engaging and immersive experiences that are both visually stunning and conceptually challenging.

Contemporary Thai digital and multimedia art explores a wide range of themes and subjects, from myths and rituals to cultural critique and social commentary. Many artists are using digital and multimedia art to explore traditional Thai culture and mythology in new and innovative ways. Artists like Tawan Wattuya and Sutee Kunavichayanont are using digital painting and animation to create works that are inspired by traditional Thai art, but that also incorporate contemporary themes and motifs.

Cultural critique is another important theme in contemporary Thai digital and multimedia art. Artists like Vasan Sitthiket and Montien Boonma are using digital and multimedia art to critique contemporary Thai society and politics, often using satire and humor to make their points. These works often challenge traditional notions of power, authority, and social hierarchy, and they offer a fresh perspective on contemporary Thai culture and society.

Many platforms and exhibitions are showcasing contemporary Thai digital and multimedia art. Websites and apps are becoming increasingly important as platforms for digital and multimedia art, allowing artists to reach a wider audience and engage with viewers in new and innovative ways.

Festivals and exhibitions are also important platforms for contemporary Thai digital and multimedia art. The Bangkok Art Biennale, for example, features a wide range of digital and multimedia artworks, including installations, performances, and virtual reality experiences.

Other festivals and exhibitions, such as the Thailand New Media Art Festival and the Chiang Mai Media Art Festival, are dedicated specifically to digital and multimedia art, and they offer a unique opportunity for artists to showcase their work and engage with other artists and audiences.

The rise of digital and multimedia art has opened up new possibilities for contemporary Thai artists, allowing them to explore new forms and mediums that were previously unimaginable. From digital photography to virtual reality, these new forms of art are pushing the boundaries of what is possible in the art world and challenging traditional notions of art and creativity. As more and more artists embrace these new forms of art, it will be interesting to see how contemporary Thai art continues to evolve and what new possibilities emerge.

As Thailand embraced modernization, its artistic heritage evolved through cultural exchange and technological advancements. Artists reinterpreted traditional styles with a global perspective while still maintaining cultural significance. This has led to a flourishing of diverse reimaginings of Thailand's traditions in contemporary creativity. Artists make references to the origins of the traditions while also providing modern interpretations through global perspectives and various mediums. Digital technologies are being used to preserve heritage, while communities are working to revitalize endangered crafts. As a result, contemporary art continues to sustain the living spirit of Thai culture, reflecting dynamic evolution within traditions of connection, storytelling, and technical skill.

Thematic and Social Perspectives

Thai art has played a significant role in shaping the country's national identity and preserving its cultural heritage. From traditional paintings and sculptures to contemporary multimedia installations, Thai art is a reflection of the country's rich history, diverse cultures, and unique traditions.

One of the primary functions of art is to reflect and shape a nation's identity. In Thailand, this is often achieved through depictions of the country's landscapes, people, and cultural practices. For example, traditional Thai paintings often depict scenes from Buddhist mythology, which are deeply ingrained in Thai culture. These paintings serve not only as religious and spiritual symbols but also as a way to preserve and pass down the country's cultural heritage.

Similarly, Thai sculptures and architecture often incorporate motifs and symbols that are unique to Thai culture. For example, the Garuda, a mythical bird-like creature that is associated with the Thai monarchy, is a common motif in Thai sculptures and architecture. The use of these motifs and symbols helps to establish a sense of Thai identity and reinforce the country's cultural heritage.

While preserving cultural heritage is an important function of Thai art, it is also important to adapt and innovate in response to changing times and technologies. Many contemporary Thai artists are using new media and tools to create works that are both rooted in tradition and forward-thinking. For example, artist Tawan Wattuya uses digital painting techniques to create works that are inspired by traditional Thai art but that also incorporate contemporary themes and motifs.

Similarly, artist Mit Jai Inn uses unconventional materials and techniques to create installations that challenge traditional notions of Thai art. By incorporating elements of performance, sound, and video into his works, Jai Inn is pushing the boundaries of what is possible in Thai art while still honoring its cultural roots.

Contemporary Thai art is increasingly characterized by a blending of Thai and global influences. Many artists are drawing inspiration from both traditional Thai art and contemporary Western art, creating works that are hybridized and unique. For example, artist Rirkrit Tiravanija creates installations that incorporate elements of Thai cooking and culture, but that are also informed by Western conceptual art practices.

Similarly, artist Korakrit Arunanondchai uses video, performance, and sculpture to explore themes of Thai identity and globalization. By incorporating elements of Thai pop culture, traditional Thai art, and Western media, Arunanondchai creates works that are both deeply personal and universally relevant.

Art has an important role to play in maintaining cultural sovereignty, particularly in the face of globalization and foreign dominance. By creating works that are rooted in Thai culture and that reflect the country's unique identity, artists can help to counteract cultural erasure and preserve the country's cultural heritage.

For example, the "Temple Fairs" series by artist Montien Boonma explores the role of traditional Thai temple fairs in contemporary society. By documenting these events through photography and video, Boonma is preserving an important aspect of Thai culture while also commenting on the changing nature of Thai society.

Similarly, the "Khon" series by artist Sakarin Krue-On uses traditional Thai shadow puppetry techniques to explore contemporary social and political issues. By adapting this traditional art form to address contemporary concerns, Krue-On is both preserving and innovating Thai culture.

Throughout history, Thai artists have used their work to critique the social and political issues of their time. From the satirical paintings of King Rama VI to the politically charged murals of the 1970s, Thai art has been a powerful vehicle for social and political commentary.

One of the most prominent themes in Thai art is the critique of social class. Many artists have used their work to draw attention to the stark disparities between the rich and the poor, highlighting the injustices and inequalities that persist in Thai society. For example, the paintings of Chatchai Puipia often depict the struggles of working-class Thais, using dark humor to critique the country's social hierarchies.

Urbanization is another theme that is commonly explored in Thai art. As the country has become increasingly urbanized, many artists have used their work to comment on the impact of development on Thai culture and the environment. The paintings of Vasan Sitthiket, for example, often depict the chaos and pollution of Bangkok's streets, using vibrant colors and bold brushstrokes to convey a sense of urgency and alarm.

Politics is also a frequent subject of Thai art. Many artists have used their work to critique the government, challenge authoritarianism, and demand greater democracy and freedom. One notable example is the "Red Shirt" movement, which used art and street performances to protest the government's policies and demand greater political representation for rural and working-class Thais.

Art has also been used as a tool for raising awareness about important social and environmental issues. For example, many Thai artists have used their work to draw attention to the country's environmental crisis, using powerful imagery to convey the urgency of the situation. The sculptures of Prateep Kochabua, for example, often depict animals and plants that are threatened by deforestation and pollution, using intricate details and realistic textures to create a sense of empathy and connection with the natural world.

Labor rights are also a frequent subject of Thai art. Many artists have used their work to draw attention to the exploitation and abuse of workers in Thailand, particularly those in the garment and fishing industries. The installations of Jakkai Siributr, for example, often incorporate textiles and other materials associated with labor, using them to create powerful commentaries on the injustices faced by workers in Thailand.

The rise of digital art and social media has had a significant impact on the way that Thai artists address social and political issues. Digital art allows artists to create and disseminate their work quickly and easily, using social media platforms to reach a wider audience and engage in online activism.

For example, the "Illustrated Bangkok" project uses digital illustrations to document the city's changing urban landscape, highlighting the impact of development on local communities and the environment. The project's creators use social media to share their work and engage with their audience, using online platforms to raise awareness and mobilize support for their cause.

Many Thai artists are using their work to create positive change in their communities. Community art projects, which involve collaboration between artists and residents, are a powerful tool for addressing real-world problems and promoting social cohesion.

For example, the "Baan Noorg Collaborative Arts and Culture Project" brings together artists, activists, and residents to create public art installations that address issues such as urban development, environmental sustainability, and social justice. By working together to create these installations, participants can build relationships, share knowledge, and create lasting positive change in their communities.

Traditional Thai art is characterized by its depiction of femininity and motherhood, with women often portrayed as nurturing and submissive figures. This is particularly evident in religious art, where images of the Buddha's mother, Queen Maya, are common. These depictions often emphasize the ideal of the devoted mother, who sacrifices her own needs for the well-being of her children.

In Thai literature and drama, women are often portrayed as passive and submissive characters, with their roles limited to those of wife, mother, or lover. This is particularly true in the traditional Thai dance-drama known as Khon, where female characters are often portrayed by male actors wearing elaborate costumes and masks.

However, there are also examples of strong and assertive female characters in Thai art and literature. For example, the Thai epic poem "Ramakien" features several powerful female characters, such as the demoness Tossakan and the warrior princess Sida. These characters challenge traditional gender roles and offer a more nuanced and complex view of women in Thai culture.

Despite the traditionally male-dominated nature of the Thai art world, there have been several notable female artists who have made significant contributions to the field. In the modern era, female artists have increasingly challenged the status quo and broken into traditionally male-dominated fields, such as painting, sculpture, and installation art.

One of the most prominent female artists in Thai history is Bencharong Nakornthong, who is best known for her intricate and colorful porcelain designs. Nakornthong was the first woman to be appointed as a master craftsman by the Royal Court, and her work is still highly prized today.

Contemporary female artists such as Araya Rasdjarmrearnsook and Pattana Chuenmana have also made significant contributions to Thai art. Rasdjarmrearnsook is known for her powerful and thought-provoking installations that explore issues of death, memory, and identity. Chuenmana, on the other hand, is a pioneer in the field of digital art, using innovative techniques to create immersive and interactive works.

In recent years, contemporary Thai art has begun to address intersectional issues related to gender, sexuality, and minority identities. These works challenge traditional norms and offer a more diverse and inclusive view of Thai society.

One example of this trend is the work of artist and activist Natee Utarit, who explores issues of gender and sexuality in his paintings and installations. Utarit's work often features androgynous figures and challenges traditional gender roles, offering a more fluid and nuanced view of identity.

Art has the power to empower individuals and communities, and this is particularly true in the realm of gender. By reclaiming narratives, challenging stereotypes, and offering alternative perspectives, art can help to create a more inclusive and equitable society.

One example of this is the work of the Women's Art and Craft Collective, which was founded in the 1980s to promote the work of female artists in Thailand. The collective offers training, support, and exhibition opportunities to women artists, helping them to gain recognition and economic independence.

Another example is the work of the Bangkok-based artist and activist Chumaporn "Lek" Tangpakdee, who uses art as a tool for social and political change. Tangpakdee's work often addresses issues related to gender, sexuality, and human rights, and she has been an outspoken critic of government policies that discriminate against marginalized communities.

Thailand's rich art heritage is deeply intertwined with its natural environment. For centuries, Thai artists have drawn inspiration from the country's lush landscapes, diverse flora and fauna, and intricate ecosystems. From temple murals to manuscript illustrations, traditional Thai art is a testament to the deep reverence for nature that is embedded in the country's cultural identity.

One of the most prominent examples of this can be found in the intricate murals that adorn the walls of Thailand's many temples. These murals often depict scenes from Buddhist mythology, with a strong emphasis on the natural world. Animals, plants, and landscapes are all represented in vivid detail, reflecting the belief that nature is a sacred and interconnected part of the universe.

Similarly, Thai manuscript illustrations often feature detailed depictions of the natural world. These illustrations, which are often found in religious texts, serve as a visual representation of the Buddhist belief in the interconnectedness of all living things.

In recent years, ecological themes have become increasingly prominent in contemporary Thai art. As the world grapples with the effects of climate change, conservation, and other environmental crises,

Thai artists have taken up the challenge of using their work to raise awareness and inspire action.

One example of this can be seen in the installation art of Pinaree Sanpitak. Her work often incorporates natural materials such as fabric, clay, and stone, and explores themes of femininity, spirituality, and the environment. In her series "Breast Stupa Topiary," she uses fabric to create large-scale sculptures of women's breasts, which are then displayed in public spaces. The sculptures serve as a reminder of the nurturing and life-giving qualities of the natural world, and the importance of protecting it.

Another example can be found in the photography of Manit Sriwanichpoom. His series "Pink Man in Paradise" features a man dressed in a bright pink suit, who is posed in various natural settings around Thailand. The man's bright pink suit serves as a stark contrast to the natural beauty of the landscapes, highlighting the impact of human activity on the environment.

Environmental art is becoming increasingly popular in Thailand, as artists seek to engage the public in conversations about the natural world and our role in protecting it. One example of this can be found in the work of Prateep Kochabua, who creates large-scale installations using recycled materials. His work often features animals and plants made from discarded plastic bottles, cans, and other materials, highlighting the impact of consumer culture on the environment.

Another example can be found in the "Bangkok Green Lung" project, which aims to transform abandoned spaces in the city into green public parks. The project involves local artists, who work with the community to create installations and murals that reflect the natural beauty of the area and raise awareness about the importance of green spaces in urban environments.

Art can be a powerful tool for social and environmental change, and many Thai artists are using their work to galvanize action on sustainability crises. This form of activism, known as "artivism," combines art and activism to create a powerful voice for positive change.

One example of this can be found in the work of the Land Foundation, a non-profit organization that supports artists working on environmental and social issues. The foundation provides artists with the resources and support they need to create works that address pressing environmental concerns, such as deforestation, pollution, and climate change.

Another example can be found in the work of the artist collective "We Are Water," which uses art and storytelling to raise awareness about the importance of water conservation.

The collective creates installations and performances that engage the public in conversations about water, and promote sustainable practices such as rainwater harvesting and wastewater treatment.

Thai art has a long history of exploring evolving cultural identities and societal issues from diverse perspectives. Today, contemporary creativity continues to use art as a platform for commentary and activism on pressing matters. Understanding the commentary in art sheds light on the evolving Thai identity and society. Artists both preserve cultural pride amidst modernization and address urgent challenges through diverse perspectives. Globalized technologies spread socio-political discourses to wider audiences.

Communities across the globe draw lessons from Thailand's dynamic artistic traditions, which serve as a means of cultural preservation through innovative self-expression. As a result, art sustains living connections between heritage, landscape, and identities across Thailand.

Prominent Artists

Thailand has nurtured an endless succession of gifted individuals whose skill and vision have left an indelible imprint on the realm of the visual arts. While certain adepts attained heights of renown for refining techniques that originated in more distant eras, others applied their talents to reflecting the social intricacies of their own time. Still, others have peered into the future, synthesizing past and present to forge novel forms of expression. This discussion profiles a selection of Thai artists – both historical and contemporary – who through their unique works have enriched humanity's aesthetic heritage and expanded discourse on matters both secular and profound.

Silpa Bhirasri arrived in Thailand in the 1920s bearing the wisdom of training in Italy and Greece at the dawn of the modern era. Recognizing how innovations in the West threatened to obscure centuries-old Southeast Asian practices, he established the first institution dedicated to systematic art instruction and preservation of cultural patrimony. Through teaching techniques intertwined with philosophical grounding, Bhirasri nurtured generations of pupils in techniques both established and innovative. His life's work safeguarded styles dating to

Sukhothai while instilling principles of academic rigor that have since blossomed into new forms.

Active in the 15th century was Maitrichit, a masterful painter renowned for contributions to the depiction of Jataka tales and folklore across temple murals. Through an intimate understanding of narrative and character, Maitrichit brought these ancient fables to life with extraordinary vividness and psychological acuity. His illustrations transmitted moral lessons while capturing the textures of everyday existence with warmth, humor, and sensitivity. Maitrichit's original illustrations remain cherished for preserving a slice of Thailand's rich storytelling heritage in its oldest documentary forms.

Suthon excelled as a sculptor during the nascent Sukhothai dynasty, playing a pivotal role in refining representations of the Buddha through attentiveness to subtle nuances of posture and expression. With refined sensitivities, Suthon struck an ideal balance between anatomical accuracy, meditative composure, and spiritual majesty. His renowned works established canons that subsequent generations have followed and reinterpreted, ensuring the timeless veneration of the Enlightened One across the Thai arts.

The 20th century saw figures like Sulak Sivaraksa emerge as creative agents of social change. Through installation, performance, and writing, Sulak has fearlessly critiqued corruption alongside movements threatening cultural and environmental welfare. Refusing dogmatism, his multi-faceted works address conflicts peacefully through empathy, compassion, and moral courage. For decades Sulak has stood as Thailand's leading proponent of engaged Buddhism and participatory democracy.

Natee Utarit crafted figurative sculptures exploring themes of sexuality, politics, and the fluid boundaries of identity. While confronting taboos, he infused works with subtle wit and beauty that disarm censorship. Rejecting objectification, Natee honored humanity in all its complexity with graceful realism. His evocative figures shed light on aspects of Thai society often obscured, communicating essential truths through aesthetic means.

Thawan Duchanee has garnered worldwide acclaim for ceramic vessels and vessels fusing traditional glazing techniques with postmodern forms. Whether reviving practices from Thailand's past or deconstructing them innovatively, Thawan's works engage in respectful dialogue between antique and contemporary aesthetics. Possessing profound technical mastery and imagination, he expands conceptual possibilities for an ancient medium while keeping it rooted in cultural inheritance. Thawan exemplifies how honoring tradition permits its gradual, organic evolution.

The new millennium continues cultivating expressive individuals attuned to pressing issues. Araya Rasdjarmrearnsook creates installations addressing the erasure of cultural memory and the fragility of collective narratives. Using artifacts and new media, her works prompt reflection on the constructive and fluidity of identities in a globalized era.

Korakrit Arunanondchai applies lens-based media, video, and virtual realities to explore the mediation of subjective experience. In multimedia pieces navigating online culture and virtual architecture, he contemplates how technology shapes consciousness and communal bonds. Korakrit's technical wizardry is matched by a probing intellect whose inquiries span science, philosophy, and social relations.

Painter Chumpon Apisuk portrays urban landscapes and queer identities with candid empathy. His colorful figurative works, infused with nostalgia and wry humor, give faces to marginalized communities in manners sensitively bypassing prejudice or provocation. Chumpon conveys lived realities with care, beauty, and emotional truthfulness that cultivate understanding across differences.

Several artists were kind enough to share perspectives on their evolving practices and visions for Thai art's future directions. All affirmed carrying forward invaluable techniques and philosophies from preceding eras remains interwoven with social responsibilities as commentators and peacemakers. Several voiced hope that younger generations might amplify discussion on issues most pressingly needing address, from environmental crises to political reform, in creative works bridging communities.

All concurred that honoring cultural roots demands perpetual reinvention and questioning of ossified beliefs. To survive changing times, the visual arts must remain sites of respectful discourse where individuals of all backgrounds feel empowered to contribute unique voices. Only through open-minded exchange, it was remarked, can artistry and society jointly progress in wisdom.

Perhaps the surest guidance remains the recollection that humanity everywhere shares more in common than differences apparent - a truth timeless works of beauty in any tradition ultimately serve to reiterate.

The visionaries altered traditional paths, while still respecting their origins. Today's artists freely draw inspiration from their work, updating perspectives to address modern issues. Understanding their pioneering impacts offers insight into the dynamic interplay between rooted evolution and global exchange that forms the core of Thailand's artistic vitality. Their influences help preserve heritage through adaptive reinterpretation.

Future Directions

The influx of foreign ideas in current times inevitably alters practices once confined within national borders. Yet globalization need not imply loss of uniqueness but rather presents endless opportunities for synthesis. Today's artists amalgamate influences with more facility than ever, tailoring external techniques to indigenous aesthetics in manners retaining the local soul. Hybrid forms now emerge organically at points where distinct lineages are encountered.

Simultaneously, pervasive technologies transform methods of both development and dissemination. Digital paintbrushes allow reimagining of antique styles from any locale. Audiences worldwide may appreciate crafts traditionally viewable only through travel. Live-streamed teachings make archaic practices accessible wherever an internet connection exists. While certain skills lose prominence, others thrive on machines that vastly magnify creators' reach across the planet. Change remains constant, yet civilization's artistic expressions survive by adapting gracefully to each new medium.

Online platforms grant exposure and income to artisans formerly reliant on proximity to populous centers. E-commerce alleviate costly overhead while casting marketing nets far wider than physical shops permit. Crowdfunding further democratizes financing, empowering practitioners irrespective of background to find backing worldwide. Technology opens avenues for traditional talents to flourish on their own merits.

Simulators also allow experimenting with otherworldly forms that bend natural rules. Virtual and augmented realities merge digital draftsmanship with Thailand's revered designs in supernatural syntheses beguiling the senses. Crafts once fixed in pigment or stone flow unrestrained through fantastical electronic vistas. While certain techniques translate imperfectly to new domains, inventive melding of pixel and practice reenergizes cultural treasures for audiences globally.

Technological tools similarly preserve endangered skills via comprehensive archives accessible to remote communities. Texts, catalogs, and interactions preserve subtleties that risk disappearance with the passing of sole experts. Digitization ensures craft lineages outlive individual artisans by circulating ancestral practices digitally between generations. Information technologies thus safeguard vital aspects of intangible cultural heritage for eternity.

Inasmition of global interconnectivity introduces challenges of maintaining definitive identities amid boundless hybridities. Certain purists fight to shield traditions from outside change, yet rigid separation risks practices becoming museum pieces detached from modern realities. A balanced course permits innovation stimulating revival beside steadfast conservation of heritage.

Commercial demands also strain the self-sufficiency of once-place-based crafts. Mass replication endangers authentic production modes yet fulfills growing demand. Ethical considerations arise regarding control and compensation relating to creative works commodified at scale. Protecting artisans necessitates nuanced supervision of intellectual property adapting to the digital domain.

Formal pedagogy also faces reconstruction with diminished prospects for careers solely in classical disciplines. Revitalizing art education demands reinventing transmission methods and engaging youths raised on screen-based stimulation. Integrating digital tools perceivable to new generations may inspire passions for ancestral talents transmitted intergenerationally for aeons.

Technological mediums expand audiences globally for Thai arts while preserving endangered fragile forms. E-markets yield supplementary income supporting artisan communities. Social sharing inspires admiration and emulation of neglected styles abroad. Online exposure attracts students worldwide to revitalized training incorporating both digital and conventional methodologies.

Partnerships through virtual platforms foster cultural diplomacy and exchange. Live-streamed workshops and exhibitions inspire appreciation of diversity in humanity's shared aesthetic heritage. Communities separated geographically strengthen philosophical and artistic bonds. International networks formed online may blossom into physical cooperation if open-mindedness and goodwill prevail between people.

In Thailand, the master-apprentice model has long been a cornerstone of artistic education, transmitting time-honored techniques and knowledge from generation to generation.

This traditional method of learning not only serves to preserve the integrity of art forms but also cultivates a deep sense of respect and reverence for the cultural heritage that each artist inherits. By fostering mentoring relationships between established masters and aspiring apprentices, the master-apprentice model ensures that the skills, techniques, and philosophies underpinning Thai arts are passed down with fidelity and care.

To further support the preservation of Thai arts, community learning programs have emerged as a vital force in revitalizing artistic traditions at the grassroots level. These programs often take the form of workshops, classes, and other educational initiatives, which bring together artists, craftspeople, and community members to share their knowledge and expertise. By fostering a sense of collaboration and collective ownership over Thailand's artistic heritage, these programs help to ensure that traditional art forms remain an integral part of the nation's cultural fabric.

As the world becomes increasingly digitized, the need to catalog and preserve Thailand's artistic knowledge in a readily accessible format becomes ever more pressing. By documenting and digitizing the techniques, motifs, and philosophies underpinning traditional art forms, scholars and cultural institutions can help to ensure that this valuable cultural heritage is not lost to the ravages of time. Moreover, by making this information widely available, these efforts can serve to inspire new generations of artists, who can draw upon this wealth of knowledge to create innovative works that both honor and build upon the traditions that have come before.

One of the key challenges facing traditional art forms in Thailand is the need to adapt to a rapidly changing cultural landscape. By reimagining and reinventing time-honored techniques, materials, and motifs, contemporary artists are finding innovative ways to ensure that traditional art forms remain relevant and engaging in the modern era. For example, the ancient art of weaving has been infused with new life through the incorporation of non-traditional materials, such as recycled plastics and industrial fibers, while ceramicists are experimenting with unconventional forms and glazes to create striking, contemporary works. Similarly, the traditional art of puppetry has been revitalized through the use of modern storytelling techniques, multimedia elements, and cutting-edge technology, captivating new audiences and breathing new life into this storied art form.

In addition to adapting traditional techniques and materials, contemporary Thai artists are also exploring the use of hybrid techniques and nontraditional media to create works that transcend cultural boundaries and challenge conventional notions of art. By combining elements of Thai, Western, and other global art forms, these artists are creating a new visual language that reflects the complexities and contradictions of modern life. Moreover, by embracing nontraditional media, such as video, installation, and performance art, they are expanding the possibilities of artistic expression and engaging new audiences in the process.

To ensure the continued vitality of Thai arts, it is essential to support the artists who serve as the living bearers of this cultural heritage. One way to do this is through the provision of residencies, grants, and other forms of financial support, which enable artists to devote themselves full-time to their craft and to explore new artistic frontiers. Additionally, public recognition of living masters through awards, exhibitions, and other forms of acknowledgment serves to raise the profile of traditional arts and to inspire future generations of artists.

In addition to supporting established artists, it is also crucial to nurture the next generation of tradition-bearers, who will carry the torch of Thai arts into the future. This can be achieved through mentorship programs, which pair young artists with established masters, providing them with the guidance, support, and encouragement they need to develop their skills and artistic vision. By fostering a culture of mentorship, Thailand can ensure that its artistic heritage is passed down with care and reverence, while also encouraging the innovation and experimentation that will keep these traditions vital and relevant in the years to come.

As Thailand grapples with the dual challenges of preserving its artistic heritage and fostering innovation, it is essential to adopt a dynamic approach to conservation that allows art to remain relevant and engaging in a rapidly changing world. This can be achieved through a variety of means, including the incorporation of contemporary themes, techniques, and materials into traditional art forms, as well as the promotion of interdisciplinary collaboration and cross-cultural exchange. By embracing change and fostering a spirit of innovation, Thailand can ensure that its artistic traditions continue to evolve and thrive while remaining firmly rooted in the rich cultural soil from which they sprang.

While it is essential to preserve and honor the traditions that have shaped Thailand's artistic heritage, it is equally important to encourage artists to push boundaries, challenge conventions, and explore new artistic territories. By fostering an innovative spirit and providing artists with the freedom and support they need to experiment and take risks, Thailand can ensure that its artistic traditions continue to evolve and grow while remaining true to the cultural values and philosophies that underpin them.

To ensure the continued vitality of Thailand's artistic heritage, it is essential for individuals, organizations, and institutions to work together in a spirit of collaboration and partnership. This can take many forms, including the sharing of resources, expertise, and knowledge, as well as the development of joint initiatives and programs aimed at preserving and promoting traditional arts. By pooling their collective strengths and working towards a common goal, these various stakeholders can help to ensure that Thailand's artistic legacy remains a vibrant and integral part of the nation's cultural identity.

To sustain Thailand's artistic heritage, it is also crucial to engage the public and foster a deep appreciation for the richness and diversity of the nation's art forms. This can be achieved through a variety of means, including exhibitions, performances, workshops, and educational programs, which aim to raise awareness, stimulate interest, and deepen understanding of Thai arts. By engaging the public in this way, Thailand can ensure that its artistic traditions are not only preserved but also celebrated and cherished by future generations.

By experimenting with hybrid techniques and nontraditional media, Thai artists can push the boundaries of their craft and engage new audiences, while remaining grounded in the cultural roots that give their work depth and meaning. Through residencies, grants, and public recognition, living masters can be honored and supported, while the next generation of tradition-bearers is nurtured and mentored.

Ultimately, the sustainability of Thailand's artistic heritage depends on the collective efforts of artists, educators, cultural institutions, and the public. By working together to preserve and promote traditional arts, while also fostering innovation and creativity, Thailand can ensure that its rich artistic legacy continues to evolve and inspire, enriching the lives of its people and enhancing its standing on the global stage.

In this endeavor, it is essential to adopt a nuanced and multifaceted approach, recognizing that the preservation of cultural heritage is not a static or one-dimensional process. Rather, it is a dynamic and ongoing endeavor, requiring a delicate balance between tradition and innovation, conservation and evolution.

For instance, while the master-apprentice model remains a vital means of transmitting artistic knowledge and skills, it must also adapt to the changing realities of the modern world. This might involve incorporating new technologies and teaching methods or expanding the scope of the apprenticeship to include exposure to contemporary art forms and practices.

Similarly, while community learning programs play a crucial role in revitalizing artistic traditions at the grassroots level, they must also be sensitive to the needs and aspirations of local communities. This might involve tailoring programs to address specific cultural or socioeconomic contexts or incorporating elements of popular culture and contemporary life to make the learning experience more engaging and relevant.

Thai artists must be encouraged to push the boundaries of their craft, experimenting with new techniques, materials, and media, while remaining grounded in the cultural roots that give their work depth and meaning. This might involve collaborating with artists from other disciplines or cultures or incorporating elements of contemporary life and popular culture into traditional art forms.

Balancing conservation and evolution is a delicate and ongoing process, requiring a nuanced and adaptive approach. By fostering innovation alongside respect for cultural roots, Thailand can ensure that its artistic heritage remains a vital and dynamic force, capable of evolving and adapting to the changing needs and realities of the modern world.

The preservation and innovation of Thailand's artistic heritage is a complex and multifaceted endeavor, requiring the collective efforts of artists, educators, cultural institutions, and the public. By adopting a dynamic and adaptive approach, and fostering a spirit of collaboration and partnership, Thailand can ensure that its rich artistic legacy continues to evolve and inspire, enriching the lives of its people and enhancing its standing on the global stage. Through the dual pillars of preservation and innovation, Thailand can forge a vibrant and sustainable future for its artistic heritage, one that honors the past while embracing the possibilities of the present and the promise of the future.

Disclaimer

The information provided in this book is for educational and informational purposes only. The author and publisher have made every effort to ensure that the information in this book is accurate and up-to-date at the time of publishing, but they make no representations or warranties concerning the accuracy, applicability, fitness, or completeness of the contents of this book.

The advice and strategies contained herein may not be suitable for every situation. The author and publisher disclaim any liability for any loss or damage caused by the use or misuse of the information contained in this book.

This book is not intended to replace professional advice, whether medical, legal, financial, or otherwise. If professional assistance is required, the services of a competent professional person should be sought.

The author and publisher shall not be liable for any special, incidental, consequential, or indirect damages arising directly or indirectly from the use of this book.

About the Author

Maher Asaad Baker (In Arabic: ماهر أسعد بكر), is a Syrian musician, author, journalist, VFX & graphic artist, and director. He was born in Damascus in 1977. He grew up with a dream of being one of the most well-known artists in the world, and he has been working hard to achieve it ever since.

He started his career in 1997 when he was only 20 years old. He had a passion for technology and media, and he taught himself how to develop applications and websites. He also explored various types of media-creating paths, such as music production, graphic design, video editing, animation, and filmmaking. He was not satisfied with just being a consumer of media; he wanted to be a creator of media.

Reading was another source of inspiration for him. He was always surrounded by books as a child, thanks to his father's extensive library. He read books from different genres, topics, and perspectives. He read books for knowledge, for wisdom, for entertainment, for enlightenment. Reading stimulated his imagination and curiosity. Reading also developed his writing skills.

He did not start writing professionally until later in his life, as he was busy with other projects and pursuits. But when he did start writing, he proved himself to be a talented and prolific writer. He wrote articles for various newspapers and magazines on topics such as politics, culture, society, art, technology, and more. He wrote books that were informative and insightful. He wrote books that were creative and captivating. He wrote books that were best-selling and award-winning.

He is most known for his book "How I wrote a million Wikipedia articles", where he shares his experience of being one of the most prolific contributors to the online encyclopedia. He reveals his methods, techniques, strategies, and secrets of writing high-quality articles on any subject in record time. He also discusses the benefits and challenges of being a Wikipedia editor in the age of information overload.

He is also known for his novel "Becoming the man", where he tells the story of a young man who goes through a series of transformations in his life. The novel explores themes such as identity, masculinity, self-discovery, love, loss, and redemption. The novel is based on his journey to becoming who he is today.

Copyright © 2024 Maher Asaad Baker

Cover image designed by Freepik